GLOBALIZING MUSIC

COUNTERPOINTS: MUSIC AND EDUCATION

Estelle R. Jorgensen, *editor*

GLOBALIZING MUSIC EDUCATION

A Framework

Alexandra Kertz-Welzel

Indiana University Press

This book is a publication of

Indiana University Press
Office of Scholarly Publishing
Herman B Wells Library 350
1320 East 10th Street
Bloomington, Indiana 47405 USA

iupress.indiana.edu

The paper used in this publication meets the minimum requirements of the American National Standard for Information Sciences—Permanence of Paper for Printed Library Materials, ANSI Z39.48-1992.

Manufactured in the United States of America

Library of Congress Cataloging-in-Publication Data

Names: Kertz-Welzel, Alexandra, author.
Title: Globalizing music education : a framework / Alexandra
   Kertz-Welzel.
Other titles: Counterpoints (Bloomington, Ind.)
Description: Bloomington : Indiana University Press, 2018. |
   Series: Counterpoints: music and education
Identifiers: LCCN 2017026094| ISBN 9780253032577 (cl : alk. paper) |
   ISBN 9780253032584 (pr : alk. paper)
Subjects: LCSH: Music—Instruction and study. | Music and
   globalization.
Classification: LCC MT1 .K4 2018 | DDC 780.71—dc23
   LC record available at https://lccn.loc.gov/2017026094

1 2 3 4 5   23 22 21 20 19 18

To Martin Welzel

Contents

Acknowledgments

THIS BOOK HAS been quite a long time in the making. It is the result of a long professional and personal journey. I am indebted to many people I have met on this journey who have supported and challenged me and who have helped me become the person and scholar that I am now. I thank my students and colleagues at Ludwig Maximilian University in Munich, Germany, but also all students and colleagues I have met during my lectures in Germany and abroad. I am particularly grateful to many colleagues in the international music education community, who are too numerous to acknowledge individually. They know how significant they are to me. They have inspired and supported me in countless discussions and helped me elaborate my ideas. Their thoughts and suggestions have aided this publication, enabling me to write a book on a topic that, not long ago, people would have thought dispensable. It is my hope that the thoughts presented here will encourage readers to continue on their professional and individual journeys and to apply and improve the ideas presented. I am particularly indebted to two colleagues who have had an enormous impact on me: Patricia Shehan Campbell and Estelle R. Jorgensen. While I will never be able to repay my debt to them, I will always aim to be a mentor for young scholars. Last, I thank my husband, Martin Welzel. Without him, this book would not exist.

GLOBALIZING MUSIC EDUCATION

Introduction

GLOBALIZATION AND INTERNATIONALIZATION have shaped our lives in ways that we do not notice anymore: the same food or fashion chains in cities world-wide, the same songs wherever we go, similar architecture in different parts of the world. Even though there usually is a touch of local flavor in everything we encounter, the international commonalities are striking. But we also know other facets of globalization and internationalization: the global reality of violence and terror by fanatic international networks, related to ideologies or religious beliefs, threatening our world order and democratic principles; the exploitation of people and resources; or the fear and rejection of globalization and internationalization, because people feel threatened by immigrants and the global economy. These and many more aspects indicate that globalization and internationalization are multifaceted and challenging, shaping lives worldwide. No matter what we think about these developments, we should face that we live in a global world, where everything and everybody is interconnected.

There are certainly various ways of encountering globalization and interna-tionalization, publicly and individually. In the public sphere, regarding global politics or economy, international organizations such as the United Nations (UN), the Organization for Economic Cooperation and Development (OECD), or the North Atlantic Treaty Organization (NATO) stand for a global world order. Likewise, there are representatives of internationalization in specialized fields, such as International Music Council (IMC) or International Society for Music Education (ISME). But globalization and internationalization are also present in personal histories. People studying, working, or living abroad encounter the challenges and opportunities of globalization and internationalization, which shape their professional and private identities.

These personal experiences have been the starting point for this book. I spent three and a half years, from 2002 until 2005, as a postdoctoral researcher at the University of Washington in Seattle, Washington. As someone who had never encountered music education in any other than the German context, I faced per-sonal and professional struggles. Realizing that I was not the only one facing these problems eventually led to the decision to turn these challenges affecting my professional identity into a research project, investigating them from a schol-arly and interdisciplinary perspective. This book is the result of this personal and scholarly journey. It provides a conceptual framework for globalizing music education. It offers points of reference for understanding, evaluating, and shaping the formation of a culturally sensitive global music education community. It advocates reconsidering and transforming music education in view of globalization and internationalization, particularly regarding lifelong musical engagement, higher education, and research. This book wants to be a guide for people's own scholarly journeys, as well as for the profession. It raises issues that have never been addressed comprehensively. It can therefore be only a first attempt to start a professional discourse about the impact globalization and internationalization have on music education worldwide and how we can use its benefits for the formation of a culturally sensitive global music education community. This is what globalizing music education means.

Globalization and Internationalization

There are many ways to characterize globalization, this buzzword that seems, as Nikolas Coupland states, to be "overconsolidated, overhyped and under-interpreted."[1] Many people use it, often just as a convenient label for certain developments, without knowing exactly what it means. Globalization can be a synonym for economic liberalization, sometimes even in terms of Westernization or Americanization. But globalization also concerns "the proliferation of new information technologies."[2] The world is connected through the World Wide Web. There is a global community; the world may even be a global village. The blurring of national borders and the increased speed of transportation support this perception. Thomas Eriksen identifies eight dimensions of globalization, describing the challenges and opportunities it provides: disembedding, acceleration, standardization, interconnectedness, movement, mixing, vulnerability, and re-embedding.[3] Some of these aspects, such as disembedding, acceleration, movement, or interconnectedness, refer to the shrinking of space and time and the subsequent delocalization, increased exchange of information, or constant drive. Other dimensions underline more critical aspects of globalization: standardization describes a process in which homogenization and comparability can lead to artificial sameness all over the world, no matter whether this is in education, food, language, architecture, or music. Individual differences according to local or national traditions disappear because of the demand of a global standard, maybe ensuring quality but also eliminating diversity and its inherent value. Mixing is, at least to a certain degree, the opposite of standardization and characterizes the growing diversity in a global world where many different cultures meet, are transformed, and represent the multifarious facets of today's societies and lifestyles. Vulnerability signifies results of the other dimensions of globalization, such as the disappearance of boundaries or the global economy—refugees from wars or economic problems, epidemics such as AIDS or avian flu, transnational terrorism or climate change—having an impact particularly on developing countries. These global problems cannot be conquered by a single national state but are tasks for the global community. If the world is one, then everybody is responsible for others' welfare to some extent. Eriksen's last dimension, re-embedding, emphasizes the dialectical nature of globalization: interconnectedness, for instance, through digital media, can lead to disconnectedness regarding the real world.

Thus, globalization is not an easy phenomenon and is characterized by opposite tendencies, such as homogenization and heterogenization, also exemplifying the dialectics of the global and the local. Arjun Appadurai criticizes oversimplified notions of globalization as simple homogenization and argues for a more nuanced understanding:

> Most often the homogenization argument subspeciates into either an argument about Americanization or an argument about commoditization, and very often the two arguments are closely linked. What these arguments fail to consider is that at least as rapidly as forces from various metropolises are brought into new societies they tend to become indigenized in one way or another: this is true of music and housing styles as much as it is true of science and terrorism, spectacles and constitutions.[4]

Appadurai emphasizes the difference between globalization and homogenization. Even though globalization might first result in convergence, it also has an obvious tendency toward differentiation, diversity, and localization. This transformation of global features according to local needs is an important part of globalization. Sometimes it is called "glocalization," indicating the merging of global and local elements.[5] This underlines that globalization is indeed a complex process. Coupland might be right when he states that "globalization is not linear, just as it is not uniformly and (ironically enough) not universally and not globally experienced."[6] Rather, it is a multifaceted development or a cluster of changes and still-changing social, economic, and cultural arrangements. It is also important to note that globalization is not a new development. Globalization has happened at different times at different places, as research in globalization history indicates, no matter if in ancient Greece, medieval Germany, or eighteenth-century Mexico.[7]

Contrary to globalization, *internationalization* is a term that does not seem to be as complicated. It is based on the notion of nation-states and aims at connecting countries and their institutions. As a term used in the business world, *internationalization* has basically two different meanings. First, it concerns a product, such as software, that can easily be adapted to countries and languages in terms of being "internationalized"; second, *internationalization* encompasses initiatives to expand and operate across national borders.[8] *Internationalization* has also for centuries been a common term in political science and governmental relations, as Jane Knight states.[9] Since the 1980s, it has become popular in education, replacing the term *international education*. Internationalization indicates that education goes beyond boundaries and is a transnational endeavor. Internationalization particularly concerns higher education. Knight therefore defines *internationalization* as "a process of integrating an international, intercultural, and global dimension into the goals, functions, and delivery of higher education."[10] This meaning of *internationalization* is supported by the American Council on Education, which defines internationalization as a "strategic, coordinated process that seeks to align and integrate international policies, programs, and initiatives, and positions colleges and universities as more globally oriented and internationally connected."[11] Both definitions underline the fact that internationalization is concerned with adopting strategies that connect institutions in one country with those in other countries. Through being linked with institutions worldwide, mutual learning, exchange of ideas, and research or teaching partnerships can be implemented.

But both definitions also use the word *global*. This raises the interesting issue of what the similarities and differences between internationalization and globalization are. While Knight characterizes the relationship between internationalization and globalization as "dynamic" and mutual, each one having an impact on the other one,[12] Herman Daly tries to differentiate between internationalization and globalization as concerns the business world. He states:

> Globalization, considered by many to be the inevitable wave of the future, is frequently confused with internationalization, but is in fact something totally different. Internationalization refers to the increasing importance of international trade, international relations, treaties, alliances, etc. Inter-national, of course, means between or among nations. The basic unit remains the nation, even as relations among nations become increasingly necessary and important. Globalization refers to global economic integration of many formerly national economies into one global economy, mainly by free trade and free capital mobility, but also by easy or uncontrolled migration. It is the effective erasure of national boundaries for economic purposes. International trade (governed by comparative advantage) becomes interregional trade (governed by absolute advantage). What was many becomes one.[13]

Referring to the original meaning of *international* as describing relations between nation-states, Daly defines *internationalization* as a connection between nations and respective organizations, while globalization merges different national endeavors into one global model. This indicates that *internationalizing* describes particularly building networks while still being based on the notion of nation-states. *Globalizing*, however, proposes the formation of a worldwide community that does not depend on nation-states anymore. Rather, it represents a new unity, based on global visions and interests. This global community is in constant need of transformations while being in search for its identity. This notion of globalizing can concern areas such as music education.

Globalization, Internationalization, and Music Education

Since music education is deeply linked to society, globalization and internationalization have an impact on it. The global market, migration, the blurring of national and cultural borders, the standardization of schooling, international student assessment, information technology, or the interconnectedness of people worldwide—all these challenge music education. To meet these new demands, music education needs to be reexamined.[14]

If music education is supposed to prepare students for successful and fulfilling lives in today's global world, it needs to help them develop different kinds of musicianship connected to their personal musical identities.[15] Young people sing, play, and dance on playgrounds, in schools, and in basements or garages; they invent or record music; they watch YouTube or play games such as Guitar Hero to learn an instrument; they share and post the music they like on social media; they compose music and share it in online communities; they produce music videos and jingles with their smartphones; they use ways of formal and informal learning; they play and try out music with friends; they have access to music of various cultures and enjoy it; they use music for mood management and for escaping into their own world; and they consider their music to be a significant part of who they are. While some of these musical activities are certainly not new to music education, others are. The constant interconnectedness, the internet, and the ubiquity of music put young people in a position where they are actors and not only consumers in the world of music. They can choose different kinds of musical activities without the help or approval of teachers. Because of informal learning, schools and teachers are losing their privileged position. Worldwide migration and access to the music of different cultures indicate that no music can claim to be superior anymore. Musical playing and musical learning take place everywhere, no matter if in front of a computer or while rapping and beatboxing with friends in the neighborhood.

In times of globalization, it is music education's task to meet students' needs and to prepare them for lifelong musical activities, whether as amateur or professional musicians. This certainly challenges traditional approaches of music education—for example, the American performance-based music education. Patrick Jones might be right when he criticizes American music education and its preference for a traditional ensemble culture and repertoire, which does not meet most students' musical needs.[16] A similar critique could certainly be applied to various music education approaches worldwide. Jones argues for a new curricular model, emphasizing "broadly applicable musicianship skills," based on action learning and critical pedagogy.[17] In view of globalization, it is important to reconnect music education with the needs of students. If they enjoy composing or playing with others, they should be able to learn the skills they need and not only what standards or curricula propose.

Music education could play an important role in times of globalization, helping students use music for their individual lives more effectively and fostering abilities needed in today's world, such as creativity, or learning how to handle diversity in everyday life. While it is important to be careful regarding nonmusical goals in music education, such as a general notion of creativity, they certainly play a role, even though not as main intention. Fostering creativity or intelligence can be a by-product of meaningful musical activities. In times of globalization, the various effects of musical activities need to be considered to secure music education's place in public schools and students' lives. However, one needs to be careful that music education does not become a mere means for supporting neoliberal educational philosophy. Jones asserts, regarding the challenges globalization poses to music education:

> The impact of globalization on music education is great, but our necessary responses are quite simple. . . . The question is whether or not we as a profession possess the commitment to live up to our responsibility.[18]

Jones is right in that the music education profession has, so far, not adequately addressed globalization. It might be time to do so. But the answers cannot be simple. We need to reconsider who we are right now as a music education profession and figure out who we want to be. Globalizing music education could be an answer to this challenge.

It is also important to consider that globalization affects not only the music education classroom, curricula, and teacher education but also research. For many years now, the international music education community has become more closely connected, starting to realize that it shares similar challenges and opportunities. While the Anglo-American perspective still dominates research in many respects, more scholars are starting to acknowledge that there are different traditions of research in music education worldwide.[19] Taking educational transfer into account is an important starting point in understanding how international we already are. There has always been an exchange of ideas, models, and policies, which was a significant factor in the development of music education internationally.[20] Without using the concept of educational transfer—for example, regarding the worldwide adoption of the Orff approach or the implementation of an international model of schooling—comparative music education misses crucial points. Additionally, it is important to critically reflect on the use of English as a global language in music education. For many nonnative English speakers, this use limits the scope of their research and opportunities for publication. This problem is not so much a matter of grammatical issues but rather of rhetorical choices, research cultures, and the politics of location in academic text production. Finally, the question of who we are as an international music education community and profession is significant. Marie McCarthy addresses this issue from the perspective of ISME and its history. She argues for understanding music education from an international perspective, realizing its common purpose but also its national characteristics. McCarthy underlines the need for a broader and inclusive understanding of music education, using the metaphor of a "global tapestry of music education," illustrating the shared responsibility and fate of music education internationally.[21] Realizing this need and acting as a global community would help improve music education worldwide. Clearly, more research is needed.

Research on Globalization and Internationalization in Music Education

When looking at research about globalization, internationalization and music education, there certainly are a decent number of publications related to this topic. But the problem is that most studies do not exactly address these issues. They take globalization and internationalization into account as only one factor while concentrating on a different topic. Therefore, when trying to give an overview of research on internationalization, globalization, and music education it is necessary to look at many kinds of studies.

Research in comparative or international music education often addresses globalization and internationalization as only one aspect, analyzing its impact on a specific topic. Wai-chung Ho's 2017 book *Popular Music, Cultural Politics and Music Education in China* and her 2011 book *School Music Education and Social Change in Mainland China, Hong Kong and Taiwan* are recent examples.[22] While the first study is focused on the impact globalization has on popular music and music education in China, the second compares three different music education systems with a special emphasis on how they respond to globalization. There are many similar studies in comparative music education, focused either on one or two countries or on more general topics. Examples include my book *Every Child for Music*, which compares German and American music education, and *Patriotism and Nationalism in Music Education*, which I edited with David G. Hebert.[23] More recently, Raymond Torres-Santos's edited book *Music Education in the Caribbean and Latin America* provides an overview of music education in Latin America.[24] To approach international music education from a historical perspective is promising, too, as Gordon Cox and Robin Stevens's book *The Origins and Foundations of Music Education* proves.[25] McCarthy's history of ISME is also an important milestone in historical research in international music education.[26]

A related field is international music education policy. Here, it is not the actual music education practice at the core of the investigations but rather the political framework, either in general or as related to specific countries or topics.

Stephanie Horsley's dissertation, "A Comparative Analysis of Neoliberal Education Reform and Music Education in England and Ontario, Canada," is a good
example of this kind of study, addressing globalization from a political and comparative perspective.[27] International documents, such as United Nations Educational, Scientific, and Cultural Organization (UNESCO) reports and Anne Bamford's *The Wow Factor: Global Research Compendium on the Impact of the Arts in
Education*, also provide an overview of arts education and globalization.[28] While
Bamford's book provides a general summary of the challenges and opportunities
education in the arts faces worldwide, there are also studies of single countries in
journals such as *Arts Education Policy Review*, addressing, for instance, cosmopolitanism and policies or global policies and local needs in Brazil.[29]

A closely related field is philosophy of music education, covering issues of
international and comparative music education. Paul G. Woodford's book *Democracy and Music Education*, for example, analyzes the impact neoliberal educational philosophy has on music education internationally.[30] Many studies on
international music education have been published in the journal *Philosophy of
Music Education Review*—for instance, the symposium "Four Pieces on Comparative Philosophy of Music Education" in 2013.[31]

There also is a decent amount of research in related fields, such as ethnomu-
sicology, investigating the meaning of globalization for traditional musical cultures, contemporary music, or popular music.[32] Autoethnographic perspectives,
as presented in Chris Harrison and Sarah Hennessy's study on international perspectives in music education and student or teacher exchange programs, provide
interesting views.[33] Furthermore, the internationalization of certain approaches,
such as Orff,[34] or specific fields of music education, such as multicultural music
education,[35] has also been significant in addressing globalization. Research on
international teaching approaches,[36] children's musical cultures,[37] or the role of
music for immigrant children specifically addressing the impact globalization
has on children's lives and musical identity[38] has also been important. Because
comparative and international music education as fields of research are still in
their infancy,[39] research on international education can be useful for improving
this research focus in music education. Particularly the studies by David Phillips
and Gita Steiner-Khamsi regarding educational transfer can help professional-
ize international and comparative music education.[40] Additionally, related fields
of research such as sociolinguistics,[41] research on higher education, disciplinary
identity,[42] or business studies regarding the global mindset[43] provide important
points of reference.

What is striking about this research is that no single study explicitly analyzes the impact globalization and internationalization have on music education
in general, even though both are implicit factors in many publications. Additionally, no study develops a concept for addressing the challenges and opportunities

globalization and internationalization present. There is also no vision of what music education in view of these new developments could look like. These research gaps indicate that there is a need for a more comprehensive study focusing solely on globalization, internationalization, and music education, thereby offering much-needed orientation. This is exactly the purpose of this book.

Purpose of This Study

This book presents a new vision for music education in terms of globalizing music education, thereby promoting the formation of a united and inclusive yet diverse global community. It is a call for consciously forming a culturally sensitive global music education community. It argues for embracing the many music education and research traditions worldwide, thus trying to overcome the often overlooked dominance of, for instance, Anglo-American music education. This book emphasizes the need for developing a pluralistic mode of thinking in music education while at the same time underlining our shared foundations and goals. Globalizing music education is not something that happens automatically. Rather, it is a development that can be shaped by people who are interested and prepared to engage in it, whether in everyday school life, research, or at the music education policy level. It depends on individuals to sustainably transform music education.

But what does globalizing music education mean? It means realizing that we are already, at least to a certain degree, international, but we need to work on becoming a truly culturally sensitive global community. Globalizing music education means transforming music education toward a united yet diverse worldwide community. It means challenging the current state of music education, particularly regarding the unquestioned hegemony or the marginalization of certain music education and research cultures. Globalizing music education means defining international and comparative music education as significant points of reference for research and teaching around the globe. It means developing a research agenda that supports the formation of a global music education community. Globalizing music education in a critical and culturally sensitive way is an endeavor of which everybody working in music education is in charge.

However, there are certainly adversaries to globalizing music education, such as the assumption that it is unnecessary and that, rather, isolation or even seclusion would strengthen the quality of music education in a respective country. The unquestioned dominance of specific approaches or scholarly authorities in one country could also be a reason for rejecting the notion of internationalization or a global community: being connected and open for new ideas from different countries could challenge established hierarchies and common ways of thinking or acting. It is important to take critical perspectives into account regarding globalization and internationalization when arguing for the development of a united and diverse global music education community. Globalization and internation-alization certainly challenge music education but also represent opportunities.

This book addresses these issues through a positive yet critical position. This means challenging possibly dogmatic or overly idealistic notions, as Uwe Brandenburg and Hans de Wit do when proclaiming the need for a "postinter-nationalization age"[44] and as other critics of globalization do regarding specific areas.[45] Thus, this book provides the vision of a culturally sensitive global music education community. This vision is part of broader transformations in music education that are much needed in view of global changes. A general vision is particularly presented in the UNESCO document "Rethinking Education: To-wards a Global Common Good?," advocating education and music education to-ward humane ends.[46] It argues for a humanistic approach to education, empha-sizing the need for situating education within the framework of human rights. This includes understanding education (and music education) as a common good, offering everybody access, and implementing the ideal of lifelong learning. Becoming aware that we are a global community, linked by our shared human-ity and the responsibility for peace and the environment, is an important global vision, which the UNESCO document wants to foster through education. Music education is certainly a significant part of these much-needed transformations.

To facilitate the necessary transformations regarding globalizing music edu-cation, this book provides a conceptual framework. It offers a theoretical struc-ture of categories and conceptual elements that can facilitate becoming a united and diverse global music education community. A conceptual framework func-tions as a researcher's map of the territory investigated, offering a specific per-spective and lens for scrutinizing a topic. It presents specific analytical categories and conceptual elements, which arise from research findings in a respective field and can lead to new insights. They guide a study and hold together the ideas pre-sented and thereby facilitate creating new knowledge.

This book proposes different categories and conceptual elements concern-ing globalizing music education: First, from a broad perspective, significant con-ceptual elements proposed are education, music, and language. While education has changed through globalization and internationalization, it represents at the same time a solution to its challenges. Second and similarly, music not only is transformed through international developments but can function as a mirror for transformations, exemplifying various processes of exchange. The same con-cerns English as a lingua franca, illustrating the challenges and opportunities a global community linked by a common language faces. These conceptual el-ements offer a specific approach to internationalization and globalization and its impact on music education and research. Their multifaceted relationship re-sults in realizing the need to think globally in music education research. Thus, there are four conceptual elements illustrating this conclusion: defining music education as a global field of research, identifying and using processes of educational transfer, and critically considering the global knowledge production and what being a global music education community means. Learning to understand music education as a worldwide field of research, not being restricted solely to national traditions, systems, and approaches anymore, is a significant aspect of becoming a unified and diverse global community. Recognizing processes of educational transfer and exchange, an aspect that already ties together music education internationally, opens a new perspective on the global music education community. This concerns likewise global knowledge production regarding which kind of knowledge the international community values or marginalizes and how the future should look. The result of critically reflecting on these conceptual elements is realizing the need for developing a global mindset, whether for the music education profession in general or individuals. For becoming international, three different conceptual elements are important: international music education policy, the global music classroom, and being global. They describe what it means to globalize music education in a culturally sensitive way.

The conceptual framework presented in this book functions as a tool and a map helping to understand, evaluate, and shape globalizing music education. The analytical categories and conceptual elements offered can be used as guides for assessing or improving the current state of globalizing music education, whether in general or in a specific country or whether concerning a specific issue such as global knowledge production. By providing these categories and elements, this conceptual framework breaks the complexity of globalization and internationalization regarding music education down into selected aspects that are easily accessible and can simply be applied to different contexts. Thereby, this conceptual framework makes a significant contribution to transforming music education globally, facilitating ways to form an inclusive yet diverse global music education community.

But even though this conceptual framework provides selective categories and elements, it offers only one specific perspective. It is important to note that the categories and elements could be different, depending on the respective point of view. The conceptual framework proposed in this book represents my perspective, based on research in several fields, not only in music education. Using an interdisciplinary approach and concepts from related areas of research such as comparative education, policy studies, sociolinguistics, or business studies seems the most appropriate way for approaching globalizing music education. The notion of educational transfer, in recent years a prominent topic in comparative education, can facilitate analyzing the international exchange of policies, models, or teaching strategies in music education. Sociolinguistic research about differences in academic discourses and writing in a global context opens interesting perspectives on the hegemony of Anglo-American standards in international music education. The global mindset, a concept originally developed in psychology and business studies, offers a transcultural and cosmopolitan approach to diversity, which can be useful for the formation of a unified and diverse global community. These different theories, when applied to music education, support the improvement of music education worldwide.

It is particularly important to realize that globalizing music education is not happening merely by chance but can be shaped by individuals and the music education community worldwide. We are actors, not victims. However, we must be prepared to play our role and make our contribution. We need knowledge and skills for addressing the challenges and opportunities presented by globalization and internationalization when implementing a diverse global music education community. Facilitating this process is one task of this book.

This book presents three different perspectives on globalizing music education. Chapter 1 investigates the impact globalization and internationalization have on education, music, and language, thereby presenting important conceptual elements for the framework that the book develops. Chapter 2 analyzes what it means to think globally in music education research. This concerns educational transfer, comparative and international music education, the international community, and global knowledge production. Chapter 3 discusses the conclusion resulting from the first two parts, that of developing a global mindset. This concerns scrutinizing what international music education policy is and the role it could play regarding globalizing music education. Additionally, the global music classroom and what precisely it means to be global, including considering necessary transformations, are investigated. The conclusion and its summary of the ideas presented offers a glimpse at what globalizing music education in a culturally sensitive way could look like.

It is important to point out what this book wants to accomplish and what it does not. It develops the vision of a unified and diverse global music education community and provides a conceptual framework for globalizing music education. This conceptual framework aids an understanding, evaluation, and shaping of the current state of globalizing music education. But it neither provides an elaborated description of music teaching or research in different countries nor offers a comprehensive philosophy of music education. It develops the vision of globalizing music education in terms of forming a culturally sensitive global community, thereby raising awareness for many aspects that have often been overlooked. Inspired by the UNESCO document "Rethinking Education: Towards a Global Common Good?," this book also argues for music education as facilitating lifelong musical engagement and learning to value diversity in different parts of professional and individual lives. The benefits of providing a conceptual framework with respective categories and elements are that it can be applied to different contexts such as countries or regions and be transformed or adapted.

This includes complementing the findings presented in this book, because they are often related to my own knowledge of German and American music education. It is the reader's task to apply the findings and the conceptual framework this book presents to various international contexts, in so doing illustrating that we are truly becoming a global music education community.

Aside from all limitations, this book addresses a significant topic and I hope opens a much-needed discourse, facilitating significant transformations in music education worldwide. It is no longer possible to understand music education only in the framework of single nations. As David Phillips and Michele Schweisfurth state, "We are all comparativists now."[47] We need to think globally to be able to address the challenges we are facing. This also concerns reconsidering higher education, particularly regarding music teacher education programs and music education research. Brandenburg and de Wit summarize:

> The future of higher education is a global one, and it is our job to help preparing the higher education world for this. Therefore, what we need are people who understand and define their role within a global community, transcending the national borders, and embracing the concepts of sustainability—equity of rights and access, advancement of education and research.[48]

This is exactly our task. We need to change music education, both in higher education and inside and outside schools, to be able to use the opportunities and address the challenges presented by globalization and internationalization. Then it will it be possible to improve music education worldwide so that it can play the role for individuals and the society it is supposed to play. This book is intended as a first step toward this important and risky task.

Notes

1. Nikolas Coupland, "Introduction," in *The Handbook of Language and Globalization*, ed. Nikolas Coupland (Malden, MA: Wiley-Blackwell, 2010), 2.

2. William Scheuermann, "Globalization," in *Stanford Encyclopedia of Philosophy*, Summer 2010 ed., http://plato.stanford.edu/archives/sum2010/entries/globalization.

3. Thomas H. Eriksen, *Globalization* (London: Bloomsbury Academic, 2007), 8.

4. Arjun Appadurai, *Modernity at Large: Cultural Dimensions of Globalization* (Minneapolis: University of Minnesota Press, 1996), 29.

5. Victor Roudometof, *Glocalization: A Critical Introduction* (London: Routledge, 2016).

6. Coupland, "Introduction," 5.

7. See Juergen Osterhammel, *Geschichte der Globalisierung* [History of globalization] (Munich: Beck, 2007); and Anthony G. Hopkins, *Globalization in World History* (New York: W. W. Norton, 2002).

8. "Internationalization," *Business Dictionary*, http://www.businessdictionary.com/definition/internationalization.html (accessed June 28, 2017).

9. Jane Knight, "Updating the Definition of Internationalization," *International Higher Education*, no. 33 (2003): 2, https://www.bc.edu/content/dam/files/research_sites/cihe/pdf/IHEpdfs/ihe33.pdf.

10. Jane Knight, "Five Truths about Internationalization," *International Higher Education*, no. 69 (2012): 2, http://ejournals.bc.edu/ojs/index.php/ihe/article/view/8644/7776.

11. American Council on Education, "CIGE Model for Comprehensive Internationalization," http://www.acenet.edu/news-room/Pages/CIGE-Model-for-Comprehensive-Internationalization.aspx (accessed June 28, 2017).

12. Knight, "Updating the Definition of Internationalization," 3.

13. Herman E. Daly, "Globalization versus Internationalization," *Global Policy Forum*, 1999, https://www.globalpolicy.org/component/content/article/162/27995.html.

14. Recent publications indicate this need for transformation. See, for example, Edward Sarath, David Myers, and Patricia Shehan Campbell, *Redefining Music Studies in an Age of Change: Creativity, Diversity, Integration* (New York: Routledge, 2017); Randall Everett Allsup, *Remixing the Classroom: Toward an Open Philosophy of Music Education* (Bloomington: Indiana University Press, 2016); and David J. Elliott, Marissa Silverman, and Wayne D. Bowman, *Artistic Citizenship: Artistry, Social Responsibility and Ethical Praxis* (New York: Oxford University Press, 2016).

15. For more information about young people's musical lives, see Gary E. McPherson, *The Child as Musician: A Handbook of Musical Development*, 2nd ed. (Oxford: Oxford University Press, 2016); Patricia Shehan Campbell and Trevor Wiggins, *The Oxford Handbook of Children's Musical Cultures* (Oxford: Oxford University Press, 2013); and Pamela Burnard, *Musical Creativities in Practices* (New York: Oxford University Press, 2012).

16. Patrick M. Jones, "Music Education for Society's Sake: Music Education in an Era of Global Neo-imperial/Neo-medieval Market-Driven Paradigms and Structures," *Action, Criticism and Theory for Music Education* 6, no. 1 (2007): 14, http://act.maydaygroup.org/articles/Jones6_1.pdf.

17. Ibid., 18.

18. Ibid., 19.

19. See Marie McCarthy, "International Perspectives," in *The Oxford Handbook of Music Education*, ed. Gary E. McPherson and Graham F. Welch (New York: Oxford University Press, 2012), 1:54; and Alexandra Kertz-Welzel, "'Two Souls, Alas, Reside within My Breast': Reflections on German and American Music Education regarding the Internationalization of Music Education," *Philosophy of Music Education Review* 21, no. 1 (2013): 52–65.

20. Alexandra Kertz-Welzel, "Lessons from Elsewhere? Comparative Music Education in Times of Globalization," *Philosophy of Music Education Review* 23, no. 1 (2015): 48–66.

21. McCarthy, "International Perspectives," 57.

22. Wai-chung Ho, *Popular Music, Cultural Politics and Music Education in China* (London: Routledge, 2017); Wai-chung Ho, *School Music Education and Social Change in Mainland China, Hong Kong and Taiwan* (Leiden, Netherlands: Brill, 2011).

23. Alexandra Kertz-Welzel, *Every Child for Music: Musikunterricht und Musikpädagogik in den USA* [Every child for music: Music education in the United States] (Essen, Germany: Blaue Eule, 2006); David G. Hebert and Alexandra Kertz-Welzel, *Patriotism and Nationalism in Music Education* (Farnham, UK: Ashgate, 2012).

24. Raymond Torres-Santos, *Music Education in the Caribbean and Latin America: A Comprehensive Guide* (Lanham, MD: Rowman and Littlefield, 2017).

25. Gordon Cox and Robin Stevens, *The Origins and Foundations of Music Education*, 2nd ed. (London: Continuum, 2017).

26. Marie McCarthy, *Toward a Global Community: The International Society for Music Education, 1953–2003* (Nedlands, Australia: International Society for Music Education, 2004).

27. Stephanie Horsley, "A Comparative Analysis of Neoliberal Education Reform and Music Education in England and Ontario, Canada," PhD diss., University of Western Ontario, 2014, http://ir.lib.uwo.ca/cgi/viewcontent.cgi?article=3204&context=etd.

28. Anne Bamford, *The Wow Factor: Global Research Compendium on the Impact of the Arts in Education* (Münster, Germany: Waxmann, 2006); United Nations Educational, Scientific, and Cultural Organization, *Rethinking Education: Towards a Global Common Good?* (Paris: UNESCO, 2015), http://unesdoc.unesco.org/images/0023/002325/232555e.pdf.

29. See, for example, Patrick Schmidt, "Cosmopolitanism and Policy: A Pedagogical Framework for Global Issues in Music Education," *Arts Education Policy Review* 114 (2013): 103–111; and Liane Hentschke, "Global Policies and Local Needs in Music Education in Brazil," *Arts Education Policy Review* 114 (2013): 119–125.

30. Paul G. Woodford, *Democracy and Music Education* (Bloomington: Indiana University Press, 2005).

31. See, for example, Lauri Väkevä, Cathy Benedict, Patrick Schmidt, Geir Johansen, and Alexandra Kertz-Welzel, "Four Pieces on Comparative Philosophy of Music Education," *Philosophy of Music Education Review* 21, no. 1 (2013): 5–65, http://muse.jhu.edu/journals/philosophy_of_music_education_review/toc/pme.21.1.html.

32. See Bob W. White, *Music and Globalization: Critical Encounters* (Bloomington: Indiana University Press, 2012); Daniel Siebert, *Musik im Zeitalter der Globalisierung: Prozesse—Perspektiven—Stile* [Music in the age of globalization: Processes—perspectives—styles] (Bielefeld, Germany: Transcript, 2015); and Huib Schippers and Catherine Grant, *Sustainable Futures for Music Cultures: An Ecological Perspective* (New York: Oxford University Press, 2016).

33. Chris Harrison and Sarah Hennessy, *Listen Out: International Perspectives on Music Education* (Solihull, UK: National Association of Music Educators, 2012).

34. André de Quadros, ed., *Many Seeds, Different Flowers: The Music Education Legacy of Carl Orff* (Nedlands: Callaway International Resource Centre for Music Education, University of Western Australia, 2000).

35. Huib Schippers, *Facing the Music: Shaping Music Education from a Global Perspective* (New York: Oxford University Press 2010).

36. Patricia Shehan Campbell, *Lessons from the World* (London: Schirmer, 1991).

37. Campbell and Wiggins, *The Oxford Handbook of Children's Musical Cultures.*

38. Kathryn Marsh, "Music in the Lives of Refugee and Newly Arrived Immigrant Children in Sydney, Australia," in Campbell and Wiggins, *The Oxford Handbook of Children's Musical Cultures,* 492–509.

39. Anthony E. Kemp and Laurence Lepherd, "Research Methods in International and Comparative Music Education," in *Handbook of Research on Music Teaching and Learning,* ed. Richard Colwell (New York: Schirmer, 1992), 773–788.

40. David Phillips, "Aspects of Educational Transfer," in *International Handbook of Comparative Education,* ed. Robert Cowen and Andreas M. Kazamias (Dordrecht, Netherlands: Springer, 2009), 1061–1077; Gita Steiner-Khamsi, "Understanding Policy Borrowing and Lending: Building Comparative Policy Studies," in *World Yearbook of Education 2012: Policy Borrowing and Lending in Education,* ed. Gita Steiner-Khamsi and Florian Waldow (New York: Routledge, 2012), 3–17.

41. Theresa Lillis and Mary Jane Curry, *Academic Writing in a Global Context* (London: Routledge, 2010).

42. Ken Hyland, *Disciplinary Identities: Individuality and Community in Academic Discourse* (Cambridge: Cambridge University Press, 2012).

43. Mansour Javidan, Richard M. Steers, and Michael A. Hitt, eds., *The Global Mindset* (Oxford: JAI Press, 2007).

44. Uwe Brandenburg and Hans de Wit, "The End of Internationalization," *International Higher Education*, no. 62 (2011): 16, http://www.che.de/downloads/IHE_no_62_Winter_2011 .pdf.

45. For example, see Michael D. Kennedy, *Globalizing Knowledge* (Stanford, CA: Stanford University Press, 2015).

46. United Nations Educational, Scientific, and Cultural Organization, *Rethinking Education: Towards a Global Common Good?* (Paris: UNESCO, 2015), http://unesdoc.unesco.org/ images/0023/002325/232555e.pdf.

47. David Phillips and Michele Schweisfurth, *Comparative and International Education: An Introduction to Theory, Methods, and Practice* (London: Continuum, 2007), 3.

48. Brandenburg and de Wit, "The End of Internationalization," 17.

1   Globalization and Internationalization

WHEN, IN 1968, the first picture of the world from outer space was released, taken by the crew of *Apollo 8* on Christmas Eve,[1] the notion of what the world is changed. The picture, known as *Earthrise*, showed the earth as a unity, rising in the dark as seen from a lunar landscape, showing the beauty but also the loneliness and vulnerability of a blue planet. It made it completely clear that the world was one, a unity sharing the same fate.

This picture, which has become an icon of our age, is certainly a symbol for globalization—a word that signifies like no other term the fears and hopes of people living in the twenty-first century. For many people, globalization stands for a specific world order, a certain economic model, new technologies, or a unified world culture. It seems to promise welfare, mobility, and interconnectedness. But at the same time, it appears to provoke conflicts, inequality, or national seclusion. Internationalization, on the contrary, is mostly understood as a positive term, describing global connectedness and the opportunities it offers. It might even evoke the vision of a unified and peaceful worldwide community. Both globalization and internationalization have a deep impact on politics, economy, and culture but also on individual identities. They put our private and professional lives in a global perspective, uncovering their vulnerability to economic crisis, political uprisings, or natural disasters. Ultimately, they prove that there is no way out, because as *Earthrise* shows, the world is one, and everybody is a part of it.

This book addresses these issues with regard to music education. In this chapter, the focus is on general issues of the conceptual framework. Education, music, and language are presented as conceptual elements, offering a specific perspective on the impact that globalization and internationalization have on music education. These three conceptual elements provide the foundation for understanding, evaluating, and shaping a united but diverse global music education community.

Education

The connection between globalization, internationalization, and education is multifaceted. It can concern different ways of learning in terms of formal and informal and new concepts such as global citizenship or international education but also higher education, long-distance education, or music education policy.

The relationship between globalization, internationalization, and education depends to a great degree on the perspective. It might look different in Latin America than in Central Europe. It is thus no easy task to approach this topic, and multiple points of view are necessary.

How have globalization and internationalization changed education? They have certainly transformed the notion of education from that of a national to an international endeavor. Education and school systems were formerly thought of as being national, rooted in distinctive values and traditions. Particularly the learning outcomes presented a national ideal and corresponded to the specific necessities of a respective country or nation. David Kamens states:

> France produced students who had been immersed in Cartesian logic and philosophy. This education corresponded to the ideal of the "rational citizen" of the Republic, detached from religion and other bonds. It was also seen as the necessary education for those who were to become part of the French state, whose job was to guide society on a rational path of enlightenment. In England students were versed in conservative political philosophy, economics and history. This was the education that corresponded to the "British gentlemanly ideal."[2]

While this description of schooling and education as national enterprises might seem stereotypical, Kamens makes an important point. School systems were originally the product of a distinctive national history, promoting certain national educational values. Kamens continues his analysis:

> In this world view curricula represented national values as well as political compromises based on political demands for loyalty and economic demands. Schooling was a cultural project of the nation, aimed at reproducing cultural cohesion and community. And the "concept" of student was also linked to national traditions of what such students were to become in adult life.[3]

This indicates that national traditions of schooling played an important role for the continuity of nations. Education was clearly a national endeavor, matching the specific demands of a state.[4]

Today, schooling has become a cultural project of the world society. Education is the main human capital and the key factor for economic and political development. Only a skilled and perfectly educated workforce is supposed to be able to secure economic success. This puts schools and universities in the spotlight. Education is not focused on "cultural and civic socialization" anymore but rather defined as a "preparation for the workforce."[5] When the market forces prescribe what well-educated and skilled citizens should know and be able to do, there is not much room for an education that is not immediately useful, such as in the arts or in critical thinking.[6] In view of these neoliberal ideals, Heinz-Dieter

Meyer and Aaron Benavot correctly state, "As we impose a utilitarian education agenda in which education is harnessed to the goal of economic fitness, we lose sight of education as a practice of and for democratic participation."[7]

Neoliberal educational theory represents today the most prominent global ideal of education. Education is thought to be the main factor for social, economic, and political success. Sam Sellar and Bob Lingard might be right when they state that an "economization of education policy" exists, as well as an "educationizing of economic policy."[8] There is a close affiliation between economy and education that could also be understood as the "instrumentalization of education for the purpose of economic productivity."[9] The focus on education for economic, social, and political development puts huge pressure on educational systems and leads to the need for assessing their success. Therefore, transparency, testing, and evaluation became requirements for education worldwide, not only for the wealthy but even for developing countries.[10] Particularly for these countries it is important to be part of the international testing culture, because funding, as provided by the Organization for Economic Cooperation and Development (OECD) or the World Bank, for example, is often connected to special educational or social development programs. International assessments can have two goals: first, to evaluate a specific educational system (for example, of a country or a state) and, second, to identify best practices and particularly successful countries whose systems and strategies can be examples for other countries. Countries whose educational system is not successful are expected to borrow best practices and strategies from others, thereby illustrating the significance of educational transfer in times of globalization. The international assessment culture in education is a significant part of globalization. Particularly the Program for International Student Assessment (PISA) has become an international program in which many countries feel obliged to participate. But PISA also exemplifies another interesting aspect of education and globalization:

> a new mode of educational governance in which state sovereignty over educational matters is replaced by the influence of large-scale international organizations . . . a project driven by economic demands and labor market orientations.[11]

The international audit culture has clearly changed the political framework of schooling and education. When countries participate in international student assessments, the organizations that develop and conduct these tests, such as OECD, have power over educational objectives and the organization of learning. The state withdraws because these organizations are in charge of governing their tests and the related educational programs. International assessments foster the globalization of education and underline that schooling and education are clearly projects of the world society and no longer of single countries.

However, if schools should prepare students to be part of a successful work-force, it might be useful to take a look at how the demands of the workplace have changed because of globalization and internationalization. Kai-Ming Cheng makes some interesting points about the postindustrial workplace and its challenges to education in Hong Kong.[12] Because of changes in workplace structures, there is less room for unskilled workers. As in Hong Kong, all over the world a professionalization in many fields can be observed: where formerly for nurses or craftsmen graduating from a vocational school would have been completely sufficient, now a bachelor degree might be necessary. Additionally, team orientation is crucial, as well as flexibility, including the willingness for lifelong learning. Diversity and integration also play important roles: employers expect employees to be able to cope successfully with personal and cultural differences. Good communication skills are necessary, too: many people have to give presentations in team meetings or negotiate with clients. They cannot expect to have a quiet life at a desk anymore. Furthermore, new structures of leadership and roles can lead to ethical conflicts or to dilemmas that workers have to face and cope with. Finally, employment is not secure, and thus workers have to be flexible and need organizational skills in order to find new occupations when necessary. Since there is no stability in the job market anymore, individual futures and work biographies become unpredictable and more insecure. These transformed workplaces lead Cheng to question widely accepted paradigms of education such as today's model of schooling. Patrick Jones also doubts the usefulness of today's schools in view of globalization and argues for a paradigm shift, aiming more toward fostering creativity in schools. This would concern a transformed curriculum, including music education.[13]

These reflections indicate that societies worldwide face similar challenges. As Richard Edwards and Robin Usher point out, there is a commonality of themes in education and educational policy around the globe regarding the need for transformation.[14] Benjamin Levin emphasizes six common topics, including economic reasons for change, criticism of schools or demands for more resources from the government, and recommendations for schools to be more commercial and market oriented, as well as standards, accountability, and testing.[15] Yvonne Hébert and Ali Abdi, when analyzing the relationship between globalization and education, identify twelve important discourses.[16] Among them is the one about technology being significant for the knowledge economy because it facilitates communication and work processes. Lifelong learning is also crucial. To be successful, everybody has to constantly acquire new knowledge and skills. Additionally, there is a need for reflective learners who are able to identify and acquire useful knowledge. This also concerns individual responsibility and the realization that everybody is in charge of his or her own professional life. Migration in terms of global mobility and the growing diversity of societies is also significant worldwide.

The quality of education in schools certainly depends on the quality of higher education. With regard to universities, the term *internationalization* is much more common than *globalization*. It describes the process of "integrating an international, intercultural, and global dimension into the goals, functions, and delivery of higher education."[17] This means that universities become international when they are part of global networks and are linked with institutions in other countries, attract international scholars and students, participate successfully in international rankings, or prepare their students for an international job market. Sometimes, being part of internationalization in higher education also means offering degree programs for international students and using English as a lingua franca. Internationalization might also include exchange programs for faculty or students. Usually, there are, as Hans de Wit underlines, four rationales for internationalization—political, economic, social, and cultural reasons—as well as academic ones.[18] Jane Knight points out that, even though internationalization has its obvious advantages, one needs to be careful, too.[19] Internationalization should build on the local context and not ignore it. It can be successful only by implementing intercultural and global dimensions into the policies and programs of universities and by addressing the specific needs of a respective university and the national and local context it finds itself in. There is no one-size-fits-all solution. Furthermore, internationalization should not be an end in itself but rather aim toward intercultural competencies and help students to be better prepared for life and work in a global world.

But there are many problems regarding internationalization that likewise need to be considered: Knight refers to five myths about internationalization, basically arguing against a superficial understanding that focuses on the number of foreign students or rankings,[20] while Uwe Brandenburg and de Wit identify nine challenges for internationalization.[21] Internationalization is more than using English as a lingua franca in degree programs or studying abroad. Likewise, it does not equate to having a few international students in a classroom or as many cooperation agreements with foreign universities as possible. De Wit, Brandenburg, and Knight underline the need for a more thorough understanding of internationalization, considering that higher education is itself already international—for example, regarding its history and the promoted academic model.[22] Additionally, it is crucial to consider that internationalization happens on different levels (e.g., the national and the institutional level), but it also affects individual professional lives (e.g., studying abroad). Similarly, this concerns different fields in different ways, because there are unique challenges and opportunities in respective areas, such as music education. Addressing them could lead to fresh insights about internationalization and globalization in general.

With regard to education, it is necessary to point out that there might be differences between internationalization and globalization. While globalization is often seen as negative, involving issues of power and exploitation, internationalization seems positive, as "the white knight of higher education."[23] It stands for moral intentions and ideals, such as peace or intercultural understanding, as fostered by international programs such as the Fulbright Program. Internationalization represents positive ideals and stands for the high quality of higher education. Brandenburg and de Wit state:

> Internationalization is claimed to be the last stand for humanistic ideas against the world of pure economic benefits allegedly represented by the term globalization. Alas, this constructed antagonism between internationalization and globalization ignores the fact that activities that are more related to the concept of globalization (higher education as a tractable commodity) are increasingly executed under the flag of internationalization.[24]

This statement questions the distinction between internationalization and globalization and claims it to be a strategic one: internationalization and globalization can overlap, replace, respond to, or compete with each other. It is important to keep this in mind and to critically evaluate these terms in various contexts.

The challenges internationalization and globalization represent supported the development of a new educational ideal. *International education, cosmopolitan, global*, or *international citizenship* are terms to describe an educational notion of intercultural understanding and "international-mindedness."[25] Particularly global citizenship education is a popular way to offer students opportunities to gain the knowledge and skills needed in times of internationalization and globalization. Global citizenship education tries to empower students to act as citizens of the world. Their thinking and their mindsets transcend the borders of nations and are based on a specific set of values that motivates them to care for the world. Today's problems are global challenges. Therefore, they need to be addressed internationally by like-minded, self-determined, and value-oriented people. The United Nations secretary general's Global Education First Initiative emphasizes significant aspects of global citizenship education:

> It is not enough for education to produce individuals who can read, write and count. Education must be transformative and bring shared values to life. It must cultivate an active care for the world and for those with whom we share it. Education must also be relevant in answering the big questions of the day. Technological solutions, political regulation or financial instruments alone cannot achieve sustainable development. It requires transforming the way people think and act. Education must fully assume its central role in helping people to forge more just, peaceful, tolerant and inclusive societies. It must give people the understanding, skills and values they need to cooperate in resolving the interconnected challenges of the 21st Century.[26]

This statement summarizes significant notions of global citizenship education. It is supposed to be transformative, empowering people to be self-determined and creative in order to find solutions to global problems. Global citizenship education should be value oriented, not profit oriented, based on caring for the world, its people, and their future. Peace, tolerance, and inclusive societies are crucial. This also means implementing human rights, freedom, and diversity. The most important notion of global citizenship education is the development of international mindedness, an awareness of being part of a globalized world where people take into account the global consequences of their actions and care about each other. These ideas are not much different from what the UNESCO document *Rethinking Education: Towards a Global Common Good?* proposes as vision for today's societies, putting education at the forefront of much-needed transformations.[27] Promoting education as a common good and advocating the meaning of human rights and humanistic principles could be useful guidelines for transforming music education in the twenty-first century.

While some of the ideas suggested by global citizenship education or UNESCO documents might sound utopian, they still provide a positive vision. The concept of global citizenship education could be a starting point for reflections about establishing the concept of a global mindset in higher education and music education. Christel Adick states, regarding the international dimensions of education:

> Globalization is a challenge and not an overall deterministic process. It is clear that national educational developments are influenced by international trends, but they are not totally determined by them. The only solution to counter the possible dangers and damages of globalization lies in enlightened persons, who can effectively communicate with one another and coordinate their actions.[28]

This statement indicates that globalization and internationalization are processes that do not happen automatically or by accident. Rather, they can be shaped by people who are interested in the formation of a culturally sensitive global music education community. There is a need for people experienced with global, international, and intercultural issues to seize the opportunities that globalization and internationalization offer. This is an important task for education and higher education. Music education and music educators should certainly be part of this endeavor. By critically considering and analyzing the challenges and opportunities internationalization and globalization pose for music education, it will be possible to use its benefits and to shape it in a culturally sensitive way. This also concerns music.

Music

Globalization and internationalization certainly have an impact on music. The constant interconnectedness, the advances of technology, global mobility, the blurring of national borders, or processes of exchange have transformed music significantly. Even though some processes of exchange have been going on for centuries, global encounters during the twentieth and twenty-first centuries have been more intense than before.[29] They often lead to transformations.

It is a matter of power and cultural dominance that determines which direction the processes of change take. Roger Wallis and Krister Malm have identified four types of cultural transmission: cultural exchanges, cultural dominance, cultural imperialism, and transculturalism.[30] They illustrate how global musical encounters work. Cultural exchange exemplifies a rather neutral interaction between one or more cultures under equal terms. Daniel Siebert recognizes Paul Simon's 1972 song "Mother and Child Reunion" as an example of such processes of exchange, because Simon combines his own musical style with elements of Jamaican popular and dance music.[31] None of the musical cultures involved seems to be dominant. Another type of musical encounter is characterized as cultural dominance, when one musical culture is more powerful than another. Karlheinz Stockhausen's (1928–2007) compositions "Hymnen" (1966–1967) and "Telemusik" (1966), combining elements of electronic music and musics of the world, could be seen as works illustrating cultural hegemony, interpreted as either cultural dominance or cultural imperialism.[32] But cultural imperialism can also concern dependency on the global music market regarding musical styles and decisions. Siebert characterizes the impact Simon had on the South African choir Ladysmith Black Mambazo, with whom he produced his album *Graceland* (1986), as such a relationship.[33] The global American popular music culture is often seen as an attempt at cultural imperialism, trying to marginalize or extinguish other cultures. Finally, transculturalism describes a communal global culture merging different musical cultures, as can be exemplified by the genre of world music.

Processes of cultural exchange can happen in various ways. Denis-Constant Martin points out that in some centuries slavery played an important role in the dissemination of certain kinds of music, particularly in territory conquered by Europeans such as North or South America, South Africa, or the Caribbean. He states that "the spread of certain phenomena, including musical phenomena, throughout the planet is linked to systems of oppression and the inextricable strategies of resistance, accommodation, and power they have brought into being and continue to produce."[34] This indicates that the development of some musical genres or styles is closely related to the worldwide history of violence and oppression. The development of American popular music in North America, whether the minstrels or musical forms derived from the blues, is a well-known example of the connection between oppression, resistance, and musical transformations. But even though oppressors enslaved people and forced them to other countries, issues of dominance related to cultural exchange are complex. Within the realm of music, power relations can be different than in societies in general. The music of oppressed people can be more powerful than the music of the oppressors and dominate cultural changes.

The impact that Afro-American music has had on the global culture for more than a hundred years is a convincing argument for the complexity of musical encounters and multifaceted power relations. This underlines the need for more thorough considerations with regard to musical exchanges, which might also concern oversimplified notions of musical imperialism. It is tempting to equate political structures of imperialism with cultural ones. While certainly in many countries the music of some cultures was marginalized or even extinguished, this does not necessarily have to be the case in general. Most often, American popular music is thought to be an example of a global music culture exemplifying cultural imperialism. Being globally distributed by the media, American popular music seems to illustrate that one dominant musical culture leads to worldwide homogenization. It might also exemplify the assumption that globalization equals Americanization, implementing the American culture worldwide.[35] But popular music in particular indicates that the notion of cultural imperialism and global homogenization is not as simple as it seems. John O'Flynn emphasizes that, even though a global music market dominates musical life and business worldwide, "the idea of nations has not been consumed by globality but is in fact part of it."[36] National charts still show the musical interest of people in various countries, even though the music presented might be part of the global music culture. Additionally, international musical genres such as hip-hop are created in any language, thereby also incorporating elements of different musical traditions. In many musical genres and styles, the notion of musical imperialism and international homogenization is not as simple as it seems. Often, complex processes of exchange, as results of networks of musicians, have opened up these structures and exemplify the complexity of globalization.[37] Since the notion of cultural imperialism is too superficial and does not capture the complex processes of cultural exchange, some scholars even reject it completely.[38]

Certainly, the interest of the corporate music industry in a global market might push music toward homogenization. But it is difficult to control completely the processes of cultural and musical exchange worldwide. World music, even though it started out as a "label of industrial origin that refers to an amalgamated global marketplace of sounds as ethnic commodities," is a good example of these complex processes, not easy to describe in terms of exploitation or cultural imperialism.[39] As Timothy Taylor indicates, world music has "seeped into the broader musical soundscape of the contemporary West," even though it has not been a large economic success. But through the use of samples, in broadcasting, and in hybrid kinds of music it has become a significant part of today's global music world and business.[40] World music might even be the "soundtrack of globalization," offering a glimpse of how processes of exchange and merging work.[41] However, world music is not an unproblematic genre. Not only issues of authenticity and essentialism in terms of defining distinct musical cultures as cultural expressions are questionable endeavors today. Rather, world music is often thought to be "a promise that comes from the desire to heal the wounds of a colonial past and, increasingly, a neo-liberal present."[42]

This indicates that many hopes and discourses surround world music, assigning it an emotionally charged meaning. These discourses generally focus on several topics:[43] First, globalization is seen as a negative development, particularly due to its relationship to technology, the global music market, and modernity in general. The second discourse concerns a celebration of world music and rather sees it as an expression of our shared humanity, sometimes even referring to music as a universal language. These and many more discourses certainly need to be challenged, because they do not capture the complex relationship between music, globalization, and internationalization. There is a need to question the notions of musical clichés, authenticity, hybridity, or patterns of superficial listening, such as being focused on similarities to and differences from other musical genres. Bob White has a point when he argues for a more reflective approach to world music, including not only being focused on exotic sounds but being interested in the history and political situation of a country and in meeting people from the respective cultures. This would lead to a much better understanding of other musical cultures and globalization, going beyond the mere interest in exotic sounds:

> Music can be a window into this complexity, but it can also be a brick wall. It can tell us something about other people, but this requires a certain degree of personal and historical effort.[44]

Understanding music in culture and as culture, using it to develop a kind of culturally inspired international-mindedness, can be a meaningful goal for encountering world music.

World music certainly exemplifies one promise of globalization in terms of the access to many musical cultures. However, it is important to keep in mind the global music market and its interest in profit when considering world music and other genres. Corporate interests guide the global music market. But individual musicians, too, need to take into account the conditions of the global music market if they want to be successful. Business strategies, such as choosing the best-suited foreign market, developing a global business strategy, or promoting products and services globally, are competencies that many musicians working internationally need to acquire and easily can through specific resources.[45] Media and digital technology facilitate access to a global audience through, for example, posting music or videos on YouTube. Considering music, globalization, and internationalization is not possible without considering the power of the global music market, the various global players, and their interests. But musicians and listeners are not only consumers or driven by the market but also actors and play-ers. They are a part of it and can have some impact on its development.

When considering the global music market and international musical reper-toire, classical music is also an important point of discussion. While it originated in Western Europe, and some of its core composers, such as Bach, Beethoven, or Mozart, are related to the German-Austrian music tradition of the eighteenth and nineteenth centuries, it gradually became a global musical culture.[46] Since classical music has also played a significant role in music classrooms worldwide, often being the dominant music culture despite respective national or regional traditions, its hegemony has been intensely criticized as a Eurocentric approach to music teaching, sometimes even favoring only listening and aesthetic experience as main classroom activities. David J. Elliott's critique of Bennett Reimer's con-cept of aesthetic education is a well-known example.[47] Most often, a controversial notion of what the musical work is forms an important point of reference, as Lydia Goehr illustrates in her famous book *The Imaginary Museum of Musical Works*.[48]

However, when claiming that the dominance of classical music exemplifies Eurocentrism in cultural and educational life, it could be useful to revisit what classical music in terms of Western European art music really is: it is the prod-uct of intense international exchanges.[49] From the beginning, Arab and Jewish influences, as well as those of other musical cultures, played important roles. The significance of musical encounters and exchanges was one of the most crucial features of classical music. Musical encounters were a continuous source of in-spiration for composers: Johann Sebastian Bach studied French music, Claude Debussy encountered gamelan, and Karlheinz Stockhausen incorporated ele-ments of musics of the world in his compositions. Intense exchange processes played a vital role in the development of classical music. Maybe these processes of exchange have given classical music a touch of musical diversity, even though its longtime relatedness to bourgeois and high music culture could imply something different. When revisiting music in view of globalization and internationaliza-tion, classical music needs to be included as one significant product of cultural exchanges, mirroring musically the processes going on in societies in general.

Overall, it becomes clear that globalization and internationalization have a significant impact on music, thereby affecting music education. Analyzing and evaluating this impact, including considering the opportunities or challenges it presents, are a significant part of a conceptual framework facilitating globalizing music education. But also English as a global language plays a crucial role for music education worldwide.

English

Globalization and internationalization not only affect the economy or educa-tion but also communication and languages. A global language such as English facilitates communication worldwide.[50] English is the foreign language most often learned internationally.[51] Additionally, it is the official language of many countries and international organizations, sometimes replacing other languages, sometimes coexisting with them side by side.[52] But what makes a language into a global language is not the countries or organizations that have adopted it or the native or second-language speakers. Rather, it is a country's political, military, cultural, and economic power. The link between language and dominance can be observed throughout history, when various global languages dominated the then-known world. Alexander the Great or the armies of the Roman Empire had a significant impact on the dissemination of their respective languages. This also concerns the spread of Spanish, Portuguese, German, or English in relation to colonialism. If Britain had not been the leading industrial nation during the nineteenth century, and if the population of the United States had not been larger than that of any European country by the end of the nineteenth century, also having the most productive and growing economy, English would not have been successful.[53]

How successful English as a global language could be became obvious at the end of the eighteenth century. In 1780, John Adams (1735–1826) stated as part of his proposal for an American language academy:

> English is destined to be in the next and succeeding centuries more generally the language of the world than Latin was in the last or French is in the present age. The reason of this is obvious, because the increasing population in America, and their universal connection and correspondence with all nations will, aided by the influence of England in the world, whether great or small, force their language into general use, in spite of all the obstacles that may be thrown in their way, if any such there should be.[54]

Adams's assumption proved to be right. He also makes an interesting point when stating that America would eventually "force" its language into "general use." This already implies a tendency toward linguistic imperialism, when necessary. German philologist Jakob Grimm (1785–1863) supports Adams's statement. He writes in 1851:

> Of all modern languages, not one has acquired such a great strength and vigour as the English. . . . [I]t may be called justly a language of the world . . . destined to reign in future with more extensive sway over all parts of the globe.[55]

This statement indicates that scholars were aware of the growing significance of English as an international language throughout the nineteenth century. Even though, from today's perspective, this assumption might not be surprising, in the nineteenth century, in fact, it was. In science and academia at this time, German and French were still the most important languages. But people familiar with political, economic, and cultural developments clearly saw the growing significance of English. Thus, German chancellor Otto von Bismarck (1815–1898) replied, when asked what was the most important factor in modern history, "The fact that the North Americans speak English."[56]

The dominance of English in today's world is obvious in many parts of our lives. English is the language of international relations and organizations, as well as travel and the media.[57] It is the most important language in international presses, advertising, broadcasting, cinema, and also popular music. Most songs have English lyrics. In many fields, English facilitates access to the world's knowledge, whether in sciences or the humanities. Therefore, English is often the first foreign language students learn. In some countries, such as Singapore, English is the official language that is spoken in public and schools. In many countries, English is taught in international schools, no matter what the country's native language is. International conferences, journals, and everyday communication between scholars of different countries are often conducted in English. The same concerns the business world. The internet and increased air traffic, as clear indicators of globalization, have facilitated the development of English as a global language. Countries where people speak different languages are not as far away as before. Communication via e-mail or Skype also brings together people of different native languages who have to find a common language, which in most cases is English.

However, the use of English as a global language is not unproblematic. There is a fear that the dominance of English might lead to a monolingual world by extinguishing other languages. This topic has been popular in debates in sociolinguistics and also in higher education. There are two perspectives on it, one identifying the English language as "an evil and threatening creature,"[58] and another, more neutral position recognizing English as a useful tool for international communication. Regarding the first point of view, claiming English to be evil, researchers sometimes use interesting metaphors: English is thought to be a "killer language," "Lingua Frankensteinia," "Tyrannosaurus Rex," or "Hydra."[59] These personifications of English, understanding it almost as a living organism, were common conceptualizations of language in the nineteenth century. Today, they seem outdated. But in view of the global hegemony of English and the fear of marginalizing other languages, authors still refer to them. Robert Phillipson asserts:

> English may be seen as a kind of a linguistic cuckoo, taking over where other breeds of language have historically nested and acquired territorial rights, and obliging non-native speakers of English to acquire the behavioral habits and linguistic forms of English.[60]

This statement underlines that critics of English as a global language sometimes assign to English the intentions of a living being, as the metaphor of cuckoo implies. English, however, is not an aggressive animal, trying to destroy other breeds. Rather, English as a global language is only a tool facilitating communication. It does not aim actively at extinguishing other languages. But in higher education, the idea of English as a global language is still controversial, especially in Germany.[61] Many academics fear that the frequent use of English in universities could lead to problems in scholarly communication, particularly regarding the dominance of English native speakers and German as an academic language, neglecting the development of new terminology. While the situation certainly differs in respective fields of research—for instance, the use of English in the natural sciences certainly being more prominent and accepted than in the humanities—it is crucial to raise awareness of this issue. It is also important to apply some of the discussion's arguments to music education.[62]

However, in view of the debates about the dominance of English as a global language, it is important to stress that the kind of English that is most often spoken worldwide is English as a lingua franca (ELF), a kind of international English. It is an artificial language, sometimes limited, not offering all the opportunities for semantic differentiation that native languages offer. Alan Firth describes English as a lingua franca as "a contact language between persons who share neither a common native tongue nor a common (national) culture, and for whom English is the chosen foreign language of communication."[63] ELF is a rather flexible and maybe hybrid language, influenced by the native languages of its speakers. Jennifer Jenkins points out regarding ELF that "language contact is the driver of change."[64] ELF spoken by Japanese speakers sounds different from the ELF of South Americans, being influenced by the structures of the native languages of the speakers and the specific way ELF is spoken in their respective countries.[65] This includes, for instance, expressions that would not be used in native Englishes (e.g., "two informations") or grammatical structures that would be considered a lexicogrammatical error. In ELF, however, they are allowed because of its specific nature. Jennifer Jenkins states:

> The bi- and multilingual majority of ELF speakers also draw in innovative ways on their multilingual resources to create forms of expression that they prefer (forms that, by definition, are not available to monolingual English speakers). ELF is thus marked by a degree of hybridity not found in other kinds of language use, as speakers from diverse languages introduce a range of non-English forms into their ELF use.[66]

ELF speakers might change English to indicate their cultural identity or just to facilitate communication, not being completely bound by grammatical rules. It gives the ELF spoken in specific situations a kind of national or regional flavor that puts the power of English as a global language and its tendency to homogenize communication worldwide into perspective. When talking about English as a global language, its impact and its danger, it is important to take ELF into account. However, ELF should be no justification for insufficient knowledge of

English in international communications. Speakers engaged in international dialogue need to improve their language abilities. But they are allowed, because of the character of ELF as a sort of artificial international language, to have certain national or regional characteristics in the English they speak, usually without seriously disrupting the communication.

ELF indicates that even the power of a global language has its limits when confronted with people, their language capacities, and their linguistic creativity. However, it is also interesting to note that ELF is not bound to a certain nation or speech community but is rather connected to the notion of imagined communities.[67] This community shares, as Jenkins puts it, a "sense of shared nonnativeness of English use."[68] Realizing that ELF is a significant factor regarding English as an international language is important, even though ELF is only a spoken and not a written language. Jenkins is right when she states that ELF is the "primary lingua franca of globalization."[69] This notion can help reconsider more thoroughly the meaning of English as a global language in today's world and higher education.

To globalize music education in a culturally sensitive way, it is important to consider language, particularly English, as conceptual element of the framework presented in this book. Linked with the conceptual elements of education and music as proposed in the first part of this book, it offers a useful tool for evaluating and shaping globalizing music education, internationally or in a specific country. When taking into account the overall impact globalization and internationalization have on music, education, and language, it becomes obvious that we need to change our perspective. It is necessary to learn to think globally, particularly in music education research.

Notes

1. The image is available on NASA's website, at http://www.nasa.gov/multimedia/image gallery/image_feature_1249.html.

2. David H. Kamens, "Globalization and the Emergence of an Audit Culture: PISA and the Search for 'Best Practices' and Magic Bullets," in *PISA, Power and Policy: The Emergence of Educational Governance*, ed. Heinz-Dieter Mayer and Aaron Benavot (Oxford: Symposium Books, 2013), 121–122.

3. Ibid., 122.

4. Understanding education as distinctive national endeavors also led to the impression that, particularly during the early years of the International Association for the Evaluation of Educational Achievement (IEA), founded in 1958, educational systems were thought to be noncomparable, just like apples and oranges. From today's perspective, this is a surprising opinion. See Kamens, "Globalization," 120.

5. Heinz-Dieter Meyer and Aaron Benavot, "PISA and the Globalization of Educational Governance: Some Puzzles and Problems," in Mayer and Benavot *PISA, Power and Policy*, 12.

6. For further information, see Paul G. Woodford, *Democracy and Music Education* (Bloomington: Indiana University Press, 2005).

7. Meyer and Benavot, "PISA and the Globalization of Educational Governance," 12.

8. Sam Sellar and Bob Lingard, "PISA and the Expanding Role of OECD in Global Educational Governance," in Mayer and Benavot, *PISA, Power and Policy*, 191.

9. Meyer and Benavot, "PISA and the Globalization of Educational Governance," 13.

10. Kamens, "Globalization," 118.

11. Meyer and Benavot, "PISA and the Globalization of Educational Governance," 10.

12. Kai-Ming Cheng, "The Postindustrial Workplace and Challenges to Education," in *Learning in the Global Era*, ed. Marcelo M. Suarez-Orozco (Berkeley: University of California Press, 2007), 175–191.

13. Patrick M. Jones, "Music Education for Society's Sake: Music Education in an Era of Global Neo-imperial/Neo-medieval Market-Driven Paradigms and Structures," *Action, Criticism and Theory for Music Education* 6, no. 1 (2007), http://act.maydaygroup.org/articles /Jones6_1.pdf.

14. Richard Edwards and Robin Usher, *Globalisation and Pedagogy: Space, Place and Identity* (London: Routledge, 2008).

15. Benjamin Levin, "An Epidemic of Education Policy: (What) Can We Learn from Each Other?," *Comparative Education* 34, no. 2 (1998): 131–141.

16. Yvonne Hébert and Ali A. Abdi, eds., *Critical Perspectives on International Education* (Rotterdam, Netherlands: Sense, 2013), 9–23.

17. Jane Knight, "Five Truths about Internationalization," *International Higher Education*, no. 69 (2012): 2, http://ejournals.bc.edu/ojs/index.php/ihe/article/view/8644/7776.

18. Hans de Wit, "Globalization and Internationalization of Higher Education," *Revista de Universidad Sociedad del Conocimiento* 8, no. 2 (2011): 245.

19. Knight, "Five Truths about Internationalization," 3–4.

20. Jane Knight, "Five Myths about Internationalization," *International Higher Education*, no. 62 (2011): 14–15, http://ecahe.eu/w/images/d/d5/Knight_-_Five_myths_about_Inter nationalization_-_IHE_no_62_Winter_2011.pdf.

21. Uwe Brandenburg and Hans de Wit, "The End of Internationalization," *International Higher Education*, no. 62 (2011): 15, http://www.che.de/downloads/IHE_no_62_Winter_2011 .pdf.

22. The American university as a combination of the British and the German model of higher education is a good example of this. See Clark Kerr, *The Uses of the University*, 5th ed. (Cambridge, MA: Harvard University Press, 2001).

23. Brandenburg and De Wit, "The End of Internationalization," 16.

24. Ibid.

25. Terry Haywood, "A Simple Typology of International-Mindedness and Its Implications for Education," in *The Sage Handbook of Research in International Education*, ed. Mary Hayden, Jack Levy, and Jeff Thompson (London: Sage, 2007), 79–89.

26. United Nations, "UN Secretary-General Launches Major New Education Initiative," September 26, 2012, http://iif.un.org/content/un-secretary-general-launches-major-new-edu cation-initiative.

27. United Nations Educational, Scientific, and Cultural Organization, *Rethinking Education: Towards a Global Common Good?* (Paris: UNESCO, 2015), http://unesdoc.unesco.org /images/0023/002325/232555e.pdf.

28. Christel Adick, "The Impact of Globalization on National Educational Systems," in *Globalisierung als Herausforderung der Erziehung* [Globalization as a challenge to education], ed. Christoph Wulf and Christine Merkel (Münster, Germany: Waxmann, 2002), 57.

29. Juergen Osterhammel, "Globale Horizonte europaeischer Kunstmusik, 1869–1930" [Global perspectives of Western European art music, 1869–1930], *Geschichte und Gesellschaft* [History and society] 38 (2012): 86–132.

30. Roger Wallis and Krister Malm, *Big Sounds from Small People: The Music Industry in Small Countries* (London: Constable, 1984), 173–178.

31. Daniel Siebert, *Musik im Zeitalter der Globalisierung: Prozesse—Perspektiven—Stile* [Music in the age of globalization: Processes—perspectives—styles] (Bielefeld, Germany: Transcript, 2015), 151.

32. Ibid., 196.

33. Ibid., 155.

34. Denis-Constant Martin, "The Musical Heritage of Slavery: From Creolization to 'World Music,'" in *Music and Globalization: Critical Encounters*, ed. Bob W. White (Bloomington: Indiana University Press, 2012), 17.

35. Timothy D. Taylor, "World Music Today," in White, *Music and Globalization*, 180.

36. John O'Flynn, "National Identity and Music in Transition: Issues of Authenticity in a Global Setting," in *Music, National Identity, and the Politics of Location: Between the Global and the Local*, ed. Ian Biddle and Vanessa Knights (Aldershot, UK: Ashgate, 2007), 21.

37. Nadia Kiwan and Ulrike Hanna Meinhof, *Cultural Globalization and Music: African Artists in Transnational Networks* (New York: Palgrave Macmillan, 2011).

38. Taylor, "World Music Today," 181.

39. Steven Feld, "My Life in the Bush of Ghosts: World Music and the Commodification of Religious Experience," in White, *Music and Globalization*, 40.

40. Taylor, "World Music Today," 184.

41. Bob W. White, "Introduction: Rethinking Globalization through Music," in White, *Music and Globalization*, 1.

42. Bob W. White, "The Promise of World Music: Strategies for Non-essentialist Listening," in White, *Music and Globalization*, 190.

43. Ibid., 190–198.

44. Ibid., 210.

45. Tad Lathrop, *This Business of Global Music Marketing* (New York: Billboard Books, 2007).

46. For more information, see Celia Applegate and Pamela Potter, "Germans as the 'People of Music': Genealogy of an Identity," in *Music and German National Identity*, ed. Celia Applegate and Pamela Potter (Chicago: University of Chicago Press, 2002), 1.

47. David J. Elliott, *Music Matters: A New Philosophy of Music Education* (New York: Oxford University Press, 1995).

48. Lydia Goehr, *The Imaginary Museum of Musical Works: An Essay in the Philosophy of Music* (Oxford, UK: Clarendon Press, 1992).

49. Estelle R. Jorgensen, "Western Classical Music and General Education," *Philosophy of Music Education Review* 11, no. 2 (2003): 130–140.

50. This chapter is focused on English as a global language. But other languages in different parts of the world, such as Chinese, might regionally dominate communication in a way similar to English globally.

51. David Crystal, *English as a Global Language*, 2nd ed. (Cambridge: Cambridge University Press 2003), 5.

52. For the United Nations, the first official languages were English and French; Arabic, Chinese, Russian, and Spanish were added later. See United Nations, "Official Languages," http://www.un.org/en/sections/about-un/official-languages/index.html (accessed June 29, 2017).

53. Crystal, *English as a Global Language*, 10.

54. John Adams, "Proposal for an American Language Academy," in *Language Loyalties: A Sourcebook on the Official English Controversy*, ed. James Crawford (Chicago: University of Chicago Press, 1992), 32.

55. Quoted in Crystal, *English as a Global Language*, 74.

56. Ibid., 75.

57. Ibid., 76.

58. Antje Wilton, "The Monster and the Zombie: English as a Lingua Franca and the Latin Analogy," *Journal of English as Lingua Franca* 1, no. 2 (2012): 339.

59. Ibid.

60. Robert Phillipson, *English-Only Europe? Challenging Language Policy* (New York: Routledge, 2003), 4.

61. For more information regarding the discussion in Germany, see Arbeitskreis Deutsch als Wissenschaftssprache, "Guidelines," May 2015, http://www.adawis.de/admin/upload/navigation/data/Leitlinien%202015%20englisch.pdf.

62. Alexandra Kertz-Welzel, "Sociological Implications of English as an International Language in Music Education," *Action, Criticism and Theory for Music Education* 15, no. 3 (2016): 53–66, http://act.maydaygroup.org/articles/KertzWelzel15_3.pdf.

63. Alan Firth, "The Discursive Accomplishment of Normality: On 'Lingua Franca' English and Conversation Analysis," *Journal of Pragmatics* 26 (1996): 240.

64. Jennifer Jenkins, *English as Lingua Franca in the International University: The Politics of Academic English Language Policy* (New York: Routledge, 2014), 36.

65. Ibid., 29.

66. Ibid., 31.

67. Ibid., 37.

68. Ibid.

69. Ibid., 40.

2 Thinking Globally in Music Education Research

GLOBALIZATION CHALLENGES OUR common ways of thinking and acting in music education. We need to learn to think globally regarding various areas of music education, particularly in research and higher education. We need to globalize music education. This concerns, for instance, realizing that global exchange processes in terms of educational transfer are important. Identifying educational transfer in music education internationally, but also using and shaping it for improving music education worldwide, can play a significant role in globalizing music education. Additionally, this means defining music education research as a global field, thereby establishing comparative and international research as foundations of our profession. This concerns likewise reconsidering what being a global music education community means, what the challenges and opportunities are, and how we can nurture culturally sensitive globalizing of music education. This certainly includes critically investigating how the global knowledge production in music education works and how we can shape it in a way to embrace diversity. Having these four issues as conceptual elements of a framework establishes thinking globally in music education research as an important category for globalizing music education.

Educational Transfer

Music education internationally is characterized by two completely different tendencies. On the one hand, there are distinctly different music education concepts based on national traditions. On the other hand, there seems to be a convergence in music education worldwide. Approaches such as Orff or the American band model are popular in many countries. National standards also play a significant role in music education around the globe. Music education in times of globalization seems to be a complex endeavor.

If international music education today is multifaceted, what could be a joint point of reference? What could function as a link? Jeremy Rappleye states that "transfer is the 'uniting idea' of the field and the bedrock of what defines our international endeavor."[1] Educational transfer in terms of borrowing approaches or policies from foreign countries is an important concept in comparative education, exemplifying transnational connections and the flow of ideas. It can help understanding music education and research as global fields. Educational transfer can be useful for facilitating recognizing how international exchange works and how it could be used more effectively in the future.

What Is Educational Transfer?

The term *educational transfer* describes a most common practice in international education: one country copies a successful educational strategy or policy from another country. The main goal is to improve the borrower's educational system. The starting point for educational transfer or "travelling reforms," as it is sometimes called, is cross-national attraction.[2] David Phillips distinguishes different stages of educational borrowing: First, there could be an international dissatisfaction, a failure of the educational system (e.g., regarding international student assessments), political or economic changes, new knowledge, or increased economic competition. Realizing problems of an educational system is usually the starting point for any interest in educational transfer. The next step would be to identify successful foreign strategies that are attractive for borrowing. If one aspect worth borrowing is found, the process of decision making can start. On a theoretical level, a government or a department of education might choose a new policy such as outcome orientation or national standards. On a practical level, this would mean studying how standards work in foreign countries, how effective they are, what should be adapted, or how they could work within a new educational system. The next stage is the implementation of a new educational strategy that depends on the political, social, cultural, and economic situation in a country. There might be acceptance or resistance. Publicity plays a major role in this process. There is a need to explain to the public why certain changes are necessary. It is also important to adapt or change already existing strategies or policies so that they would most likely work within a new educational context. To assure the success of the implementation, constant evaluation is necessary. The final stage, the internalization, occurs when a new strategy or policy is completely naturalized and has become part of an educational system other than the original.[3]

To capture the various processes of educational transfer, David Phillips and his colleagues developed so-called Oxford models.[4] They illustrate the modalities of borrowing in a systematic way. There are three important models, *spectrum of educational transfer, four stages of policy borrowing,* and *filters in the policy borrowing process,* analyzing educational transfer from different perspectives.

The *spectrum model* tries to describe the relationship between two countries—the one from which an educational strategy is borrowed and the one interested in the educational transfer. Phillips identified four different ways of borrowing, which he characterized as "imposed," "required under constraint," "negotiated under constraint," and "borrowed purposefully." They are related to different political situations in a specific country, such as totalitarian regimes, occupied countries, educational transfer as part of political agreements, intentional copying, or the general influence of educational ideas. The spectrum model tries to explain the reasons for and circumstances of transfer.

The *four stages model* categorizes the different levels of purposeful borrowing into cross-national attraction, decision, implementation, and internalization or indigenization. It offers a chronological model of implementation and indigenization, the exact form of which might differ slightly in specific circumstances.

The *filters model* explains how a policy is transformed in the process of borrowing when implemented in terms of postulating "a series of 'filters' (or 'lenses') through which perceptions or practices pass and become transformed."[5] These "filters," which transform or modify a policy, are "human actors," or people involved in the process of borrowing, as well as institutions. Their different perspectives have an impact on the appearance of the transferred policy or strategy. The phases in the process, such as interpretation, transmission, reception, or implementation, are characterized by different factors—for example, organizations, agencies such as media or publications, individual institutions, and finally, at the implementation stage, the context and the practitioners. This model illustrates that educational transfer depends on human beings and institutions.

The Oxford models try to describe borrowing as a systematic and purposeful process. But the models have problems, as Rappleye underlines. They are focused on purposeful copying, are developed through analyzing past borrowing (Germany and the United Kingdom), and are not sufficient regarding globalization and developing countries.[6] Yet the models elucidate the complex process of borrowing.

However, when trying to borrow an educational strategy, it is important to know what should be copied. Kimberly Ochs and David Phillips emphasize that there are different policy features that could be attractive for a country—for example, the guiding philosophy or policy emphasizing specific goals, such as the German tradition of *Bildung* and the intention of educating self-determined and mature students.[7] But it might also be that countries are interested in enabling structures and how policies work in the real world. This might concern the structure of schooling (e.g., funding, administration), regular processes (e.g., curricula, assessment), or teaching styles and methods (e.g., Orff approach). Borrowing and educational transfer often involve only selected aspects. Phillips refers to the British interest in the German school system in the nineteenth and twentieth centuries.[8] When facing problems after the introduction of compulsory primary education in 1870, the British government sent a questionnaire to foreign states, asking for information about their school systems, particularly regarding funding, fees, public aid, and the transition from primary to secondary education. The information from Germany was particularly useful. In the 1980s, Germany again became a focus of British interest in educational transfer, specifically regarding assessment, oral testing, the national grading system, and the status and salaries of teachers. In both cases, the British government borrowed and implemented only selected features of the German school system.

More recently, international examples of borrowing are the Program for International Student Assessment (PISA) and the Bologna process. PISA is an international assessment of fifteen-year-old students' abilities in core subjects conducted by the Organization for Economic Cooperation and Development (OECD). PISA is an official way of promoting educational transfer: the best educational systems are identified through student assessment. Nations whose students perform poorly are supposed to borrow successful policies and strategies. PISA represents a new way of educational governance by which national educational sovereignty might be replaced by the power of international organizations such as OECD and their notions of education. The educational philosophy of such organizations— for example, the connection of education and the economy—is highly influential, partly because OECD offers access to financial resources that are linked to test results. This means that a government that wants funding for improving its educational system needs to submit to the educational ideas and the kind of educational transfer OECD favors. This is certainly not unproblematic, but it clearly indicates how globalization and internationalization affect education.

The Bologna process is another development supporting educational transfer, focused on higher education across Europe. The Bologna declaration, which was signed in 1999 by the ministers of education of twenty-nine European countries, tried to create a unified European higher education area. It is, as Roger Dale and Susan Robertson state, a "non-binding intergovernmental agreement whose aims were to enhance the employability and mobility of citizens and to increase the international attractiveness and competitiveness of European higher education."[9] The Bologna agreement promotes the introduction of two different kinds of degrees in European higher education, the bachelor's degree as a three-year undergraduate degree and a two-year master's degree thereafter as a graduate degree. The European Credit Transfer and Accumulation System (ECTS) standardizes students' workload and the credit points received. Apart from these organizational transformations, the Bologna process also changes the goals and intentions of programs in higher education to be shorter and focused on employability and the future job profile. Mere academic goals such as becoming a knowledgeable and self-determined person as emphasized by the German notion of *Bildung* are not important anymore. Dale and Robertson describe the meaning of the Bologna process in this way:

> In essence, the Bologna process needs to be viewed, not just as a higher-education reform, but a reform that has altered what it means to talk about knowledge, the university, student mobility, a national higher education system, higher education as a public good.[10]

The Bologna reform harmonizes higher education across Europe but also implements new goals of university programs and reorganizes their structures. It is an example of educational transfer on various levels. It legitimizes extensive changes by the power of a political agreement and thereby relieves politicians of intense justification, including convincing the public.

This indicates that educational transfer can have political implications. Politicians sometimes use educational transfer for supporting their own interests, claiming that they did everything they could by adopting a strategy or policy that is successful in another country. Gita Steiner-Khamsi underlines that the need for borrowing can be intensified by "scandalizing" the situation in a home country or "glorifying" the state of a foreign educational system or strategy, opening a discourse that is based on illusions rather than the real world.[11] The power of discourse is, in general, an important aspect in the process of educational transfer. Some scholars associated with world system theory even state that the meaning of educational transfer for politicians and educationalists lies mostly in its power in political discourses.

Rappleye underlines that it can be useful to understand educational transfer from the perspective of theories of globalization such as world culture theory or world system theory.[12] World culture theory emphasizes that globalization causes an increased convergence of cultures. Similar notions of education, democracy, or economy support the development toward shared global models in various fields. Contrary to this opinion, the world system theory underlines that there is no homogenization of culture globally but rather that this is a semantic construction and illusion. When looking beyond the superficial observation of a homogenized culture, it might seem that the so-called convergence is only part of an elaborated discourse. The world system theory is favored by many scholars conducting important research regarding educational transfer, such as Gita Steiner-Khamsi or Juergen Schriewer. It clearly has its advantages when it comes to understanding educational transfer and moving beyond the Oxford models. But world culture theory also offers interesting insights into educational transfer, and it might be that, depending on the respective context, each one can be a useful framework for research.

Nevertheless, the notion of educational transfer offers one explanation for the convergence of educational systems worldwide. This also concerns music education, in which many policies, strategies, and methods seem to have become more similar internationally.

Music Education and Educational Transfer

Even though there is no extensive research into educational transfer in music education, borrowing has been going on for some time.[13] Particularly since the introduction of music education in public schools that happened in many countries during the nineteenth century, there was an increased interest in identifying and copying successful educational practices.

THE HISTORICAL PERSPECTIVE

There were many educational travelers during the nineteenth century, searching for successful educational practices they could copy. Switzerland in particular was attractive, because of Johann Heinrich Pestalozzi's (1746–1827) work, but so was Germany, too. The myth of the Germans as a musical people, as Bernarr Rainbow describes it, was a strong argument for believing in the superiority of German music education, particularly for English visitors.[14] A well-documented example is John Hullah's (1812–1884) and John Spencer Curwen's (1847–1916) visit to Germany in 1878. While they hoped to find superior music education methods, they were deeply disappointed: singing by ear, the use of the violin in German schools, and a general lack of instructional method was not what they expected to see.[15] While this attempt at borrowing was not successful, it nevertheless reveals some interesting general aspects of educational transfer. At the beginning of the cross-national attraction was a glorification of German music education, as supposedly being superior. This implies that the expectations were and are often not realistic. It is useful to undertake a more critical examination of the seemingly attractive educational system to avoid failed attempts at borrowing. The second interesting aspect is a glimpse at the history of comparative education and music education. There have been different stages in its development, as Harold Noah and Max Eckstein point out.[16] First, travelers described only in general what they observed in foreign countries. These descriptions were driven by curiosity and a general interest in foreign practices rather than by specific pedagogical intentions. They usually provided little useful information regarding education. In the second stage, travelers had clear pedagogical intentions and very specific questions—for example, looking for singing methods to borrow. Hullah and Curwen would certainly be the second kind of travelers. However, no matter what intentions drove visitors to other countries, these visitors were important for the development of comparative education and music education, collecting valuable information.[17]

When music education was introduced in public schools during the nineteenth century, educational borrowing was a most common procedure. One example is Japan. It adopted Western models concerning classical music and American music education practices quite early. Masafumi Ogawa emphasizes that one reason for this was that classical music was "inseparable from industrialization and imperialism, since it was imported and implanted along with political and economic ideologies during the nineteenth century."[18] Classical music symbolized progress and development in culture and economy but also questioned the value of Japanese culture. Since Japanese music education's focus was on classical music, Japanese educators had to study abroad or foreign educators had to come to Japan.[19] Therefore, from 1880 until 1882, Luther Whiting Mason (1818–1896), who had formerly served as superintendent of the Boston public schools and developed many textbooks in the United States, worked in Japan. The Japanese government hoped that Mason would use and adapt his methods and materials to help develop Japanese music education. Mason created two volumes of the first music education textbook series in Japan, basically using the material of his own *The National Music Course*, only adding a few new songs. Additionally, Mason was involved in the work on a teachers' manual, mostly modeled after his own *The National Music Teacher*. Parts of the American originals were translated and used in Japanese teacher training. Aside from creating teaching materials and manuals, he also worked in Japanese schools and could test his materials. Mason's work is certainly an interesting example of educational transfer because he went to Japan to help establish a Japanese national music education system. Through his work in Japanese schools, he could get to know the country and its educational system. By "borrowing" his own American teaching materials, he represents an interesting variation of educational transfer: he first used the original American edition, with only minor additions from Japanese music educators. Later, he included more Japanese songs and tried to adapt his own materials to the Japanese situation. But eventually, the Japanese government terminated Mason's contract because there was a disagreement about the development of Japanese music education, including the blending of Japanese and classical music. According to his officials, Mason emphasized classical music too much and created Japanese music education as a copy of the American system. He did not transform the American model sufficiently to create a genuinely Japanese music education approach.

The significance of adaptation is one aspect of educational borrowing that the English educationalist Michael Sadler (1861–1943) had already emphasized in 1900:

> We cannot wander at pleasure among the educational systems of the world, like a child strolling through a garden, and pick off a flower from one bush and some leaves from another, and then expect that if we stick what we have gathered into the soil at home, we shall have a living plant.[20]

Educational transfer can be successful only if the original strategy or policy is transformed. The metaphor of the plant used by Sadler clearly indicates this. Just transplanting the original will hardly be effective. Before introducing a new strategy or policy, there is a need to thoroughly analyze what should be changed, so that it might work effectively within a new environment. Through evaluation, the results of the educational transfer can be assessed and necessary adjustments made. Finally, there will be an indigenization of the borrowed strategy or policy.

In the transformed version, it becomes a natural part of a new educational system. This clearly indicates that educational transfer is not an easy endeavor and needs a lot of critical analysis and adaptation. The quick-fix solutions that politicians sometimes prefer will most likely not work.[21]

But it is not necessary to copy an entire music education system. Cross-national attraction can concern various aspects of an educational system, no matter if these are general structures or goals, concern the educational philosophy, or are methods. Specific methods have often been the focus of attention. Wilfried Gruhn describes the adoption of Pestalozzian principles by Lowell Mason (1792–1872) for American nineteenth-century singing instruction.[22] Mason was not interested in borrowing the entire educational philosophy, which was based on the notion of *Bildung* and cultivation as presented in J. G. Kuebler's version of the Pestalozzian approach. Rather, Mason was focused on copying successful singing methods. Gruhn points out that "to Kuebler, music instruction serves primarily for the general cultivation of people, whereas for Mason music instruction is for the cultivation of vocal music."[23] While it is most common for educational transfer to ignore some aspects, the interest being only on very specific features, this is not unproblematic. Difficulties in the implementation may occur because some aspects, such as the educational philosophy a strategy is based on, have not been considered sufficiently.

There are, however, many examples of successful borrowing in international music education. The Orff Schulwerk is a well-known example. In many countries worldwide, the Orff approach is used successfully. One of the reasons for this success might be that Carl Orff (1895–1982) created his approach to be international and to be adapted to various music education systems, even though its original version was developed within German music education. Adapting the Orff Schulwerk to different cultural contexts is possible because core features include improvisation, music's connection to movement and language, the notion of elemental music and the Orff instruments, which are not limited to a specific musical culture. Apart from these basics, there are many aspects that can change according to a specific context or cultural tradition—for example, the song repertoire, specific methods, or textbooks—to meet the needs of music education systems in specific countries. Orff intended not just one version of his Schulwerk, but many.[24] The notion of educational transfer was already an option he might have considered at the beginning.

But the Orff Schulwerk is not the only good example for successful educational transfer; the Kodály and the Dalcroze methods are, too. The concentration of core principles supplemented by aspects that can be changed according to a new context seems to be significant for successful educational transfer. In international music education, many methods prove that successful educational transfer can happen—for example, the various versions of solfège. There are many examples in international music education (e.g., South Africa, Argentina, Australia) of the successful use and development of this old method of connecting signs and movement with pitch.[25] But the introduction of methods or educational concepts in countries that have been former colonies also raises an issue that Phillips tries to capture with his spectrum model: Was the introduction always voluntary and purposeful, or was it forced on people by an authoritarian government or institutions such as the church? This question indicates that the concept of educational transfer can also be useful for the notion of decolonization, identifying borrowed strategies that signify the power of oppressors. It could be a starting point to reconsider indigenous ways of musical learning that were common in a country before the invasion of the colonial power. Informal or oral learning practices in particular might have been important. Adopting classical music as the international music standard, including the ways it is taught, can also be a rather questionable example for educational transfer. Roe-Min Kok raises this significant issue when describing her experiences as a "postcolonial child" in Malaysia, suffering from the British piano curriculum and teaching approach to which she was required to submit when she wanted to learn piano.[26]

These aspects clearly indicate that educational transfer can be a part of the problems globalization and internationalization cause. Considering educational transfer thoroughly might imply taking colonization and decolonizing into account. This leads to the question of what educational transfer looks like today, in a time of increased global flow and international exchange.

Borrowing Today

The international convergence in music education concerns several aspects. Approaches such as general or performance-based music education can be found in many countries. Classical music has long been the focus of music education around the world. Aesthetic and multicultural music education have also played a significant role, the latter owing to political developments. More general principles of education, such as being student-centered or action-oriented, are also most common worldwide. The international success of approaches such as Orff, Kodály, or Dalcroze is well known. The differentiation between curricular and extracurricular musical activities or various kinds of ensembles is also internationally similar. It is most often difficult to trace the origin of these international models and to determine if they are, in fact, the result of educational transfer. Sometimes, as Alexander Wiseman and David Baker state, "ideas . . . flow down and outward through the world,"[27] and it would certainly not be appropriate to claim that every educational similarity worldwide qualifies as educational transfer. However, the question remains as to how this international convergence in music education was possible. Educational transfer is one of the most convincing answers.

While today most educational transfer is complex, there is a famous example of educational transfer that, for the most part, still follows the principles of borrowing as explained by the Oxford models: the Venezuelan El Sistema project. Originally founded in Venezuela in 1975 by the music educator José Antonio Abreu (b. 1939), it presents one of the most successful attempts to use classical music as a social agency, offering educational and professional opportunities for disadvantaged children and young people. In Venezuela in 2015 more than five hundred thousand young people were enrolled in El Sistema.[28] The program provides four hours of musical training after school every day, as well as activities on the weekend. Its official motto, "Social action for music," characterizes its main intent: to use classical music as an agent for social justice and personal development. Abreu says that "music has to be recognized as an agent of social development, in the highest sense, . . . because it transmits the highest values— solidarity, harmony, mutual compassion. And it has the ability to unite an entire community, and to express sublime feelings."[29] While this can be an empowering statement, it is also an oversimplified understanding of music that needs to be challenged. But there are certainly more aspects of El Sistema that researchers criticize, such as the focus on classical music, the idealization of the orchestra, questionable teaching methods for implementing social justice by following "a curriculum based around the performance of classical orchestral music,"[30] or the connection to a controversial political system. However, the program was adopted in many countries, such as the United States (2007), the United Kingdom (2009), Canada (2007), or Portugal (2005). Looking at it through the lens of the Oxford models reveals interesting aspects. The starting point is certainly cross-national attraction. El Sistema represents a concept that emphasizes the transformative power of music in the lives of children and young adults. It uses music and education as means for social, economic, and individual development. But El Sistema being nationally supported and partly funded by a controversial government can cause problems when trying to transfer it. The Oxford models could open interesting perspectives on the introduction of El Sistema in countries and also highlight the need for critical reflection and evaluation. As Sadler said, transplanting is not enough; there needs to be a more considered approach. But in view of globalization, the Oxford models are certainly not sufficient to explain all kinds of borrowing, even though the adaptation of El Sistema represents purposeful borrowing, in which the copied concept and the actors are obvious.

Apart from copying models in a purposeful way, there has always been unpurposeful borrowing, or borrowing staged by hidden actors. The result is the kind of international homogenization we are used to today. The global music market plays a major role in this development. By standardizing teaching materials or promoting certain kinds of ensembles and musical repertoire internationally there are more business opportunities for publishers worldwide. Many people are used to buying popular teaching materials that were originally designed for the American or Asian market—for example, for piano or band instruments. Selling the same teaching materials for a global music market certainly qualifies as educational transfer. However, this strategy is not unproblematic, because it secretly promotes, for instance, the American band model or the same piano repertoire all over the world, implementing them as hidden international standards. National or regional ensemble or repertoire traditions, as well as teaching materials by national publishers, become less interesting.

Standards and competencies are also well-known examples of educational transfer. While the outcome orientation they represent first emerged during the 1960s, because of the Sputnik shock, standards have become in recent years a popular part of globalized education, signifying neoliberal educational philosophy. Quality management is an important task if there is a close link between education and economic success. Standards try to eliminate individual teachers' weaknesses and stand for the quality of a school system and its policies. They indicate that a school subject such as music education that is focused on standards and is constantly evaluated by students' performances can reach the intended goals. Standards policies have become some of the most popular educational policies, accepted worldwide and signifying globalization. Even though there have been many debates about their meaning, they have been implemented by politicians because they help them assure the public that they have done everything they could to improve the educational system.[31] This clearly shows that borrowing has, particularly for politicians, a kind of fascination that they do not want to give up. Steiner-Khamsi points out the political dimensions of reforms in view of globalization:

> Educational borrowing serves as a powerful means to displace contested educational reforms. . . . References to successful national educational reforms of other countries gives policy analysts leverage in pushing through a particular policy option.[32]

Politicians like to use educational transfer to justify educational changes. Borrowing seems to be a convincing strategy, often staged as the only solution to save an educational system. The adoption of standards worldwide is an example of this kind of strategy. The power of internationalization, doing what others do successfully, implies that critical reflection is not necessary. Successful foreign policies carry an almost unquestioned legitimacy when it comes to reforms in another country. Schriewer describes something similar when he talks about externalization as a strategy in political discourses. He states that "externalizations to foreign examples or to world situations . . . involve the discursive interpretation of international phenomena for issues of educational policy and ideological legitimation."[33] This indicates that the power of discourse focused on borrowing can sometimes be more crucial than the borrowing itself. It is important to sell the changes, to convince the public and administrators that certain transformations will be successful and will help improve the educational system. Without a surrounding discourse pointing out the need for borrowing, educational transfer would be difficult. Politicians know how to use the power of discourse for more than just the intended educational transfer, maybe also pushing through some of their own ideas. Regarding such circumstances, it would be interesting to use the Oxford models to obtain a clearer picture of the processes and discourses involved in educational transfer in international music education.

International Music Education and Educational Transfer

Research investigating educational transfer in international music education will be crucial in the future. The Oxford models help in understanding how it works and offer interesting insights into the processes. This can be very helpful when dealing with purposeful borrowing—for example, the El Sistema model. While the Oxford models are an excellent way of understanding the processes involved in purposeful borrowing, they have also been criticized:[34] First, Phillips developed these models basically by analyzing past processes of borrowing, particularly between Germany and the United Kingdom. It is not clear if the research findings and models are useful today, particularly in view of globalization. Second, that the basis for these models is borrowing between wealthy nations raises the question of whether they can capture the situation in developing countries. Third, the Oxford models are focused on purposeful borrowing. But most educational transfer today happens unpurposefully—or is secretly staged by hidden actors. Generally, the models are focused on past paradigms, particularly regarding notions of states and policy processes. Val Rust states:

> Most of the borrowing that has been documented has been between nation-states or between systems of education in the modern age. With the emergence of transnational conditions within the context of globalization, new models are yet to be developed that illuminate the borrowing and lending process in education under these conditions.[35]

This indicates that, even though the Oxford models explain many aspects of educational transfer, borrowing today is a much more complex endeavor. There is a clear need for new or revised models.

Therefore, Rappleye suggests revisions of the spectrum model, the four stages of policy borrowing, and the filters in the policy borrowing model.[36] His main critique concerns the oversimplified notions of borrowing—for example, in the spectrum model the circumstances of borrowing, such as "negotiated under constraint," or the actors and organizations involved. The models need to consider the new global mechanics and processes of educational transfer, including combinations of voluntary and involuntary borrowing as well as multiple transfer episodes, spatial dimensions (e.g., the specific situation in developing countries) or temporal-historical aspects, such as the most attractive countries to borrow from as they change over time. Rappleye makes valuable claims that can also help international music education.

Regarding globalizing music education, it will be crucial to place educational transfer at the center of the discussion. So far, most borrowing has gone on unnoticed, but globalization, with all the issues of hegemony, power, and convergence of cultures involved, requires a more explicit analysis of these issues. The Oxford models and their revised versions need to be adapted and used for music education. This would facilitate much-needed research on educational transfer and the global flow of educational models, policies, and methods. It would help introduce successful concepts worldwide but also allow a thorough critique, using the expertise of comparative education.

While educational transfer is certainly a popular strategy, it is also crucial to point out its problems: it should not be used like a cargo culture, as a readily available cut-and-paste solution. Just copying something that works somewhere else would be inappropriate to solve the problems music education encounters in different countries. Education and music education are complex fields but with a tendency toward oversimplified solutions. David Kamens points out correctly that "education has features which lead people to believe in magical solutions."[37] But clearly, it is necessary to fight against the search for a panacea, against the belief in simplistic solutions or in shamanic magic in international education and music education. Introducing standards in various subjects might have been such an attempt. But there are no easy solutions to complex problems. Kamens states:

> A "shamanic culture" is thus likely to persist in education, precisely because it is such an important institution in modern society but one whose structure does not make it amenable to engineering-type solutions.[38]

Educational transfer offers many opportunities but should not be used as the only solution to educational problems worldwide. More research is needed for using educational transfer in a way that values the diversity of the global music education community but also supports learning from each other and the exchange of educational strategies or policies. Even though educational transfer can function as a unifying idea for globalizing music education, it is important that educational transfer happens purposefully, thoroughly guided and evaluated by research. However, as a conceptual element in a framework that aims at facilitating the formation of a unified and diverse global music education community, the notion of educational transfer is significant. It reminds us that we are already internationally connected and can continue learning from each other in various fields. If used wisely, educational transfer can even facilitate defining music education research as a global field, with comparative and international research as foundation.

Comparative and International Music Education

Comparative and international education have long been fields of research on the margins, considered exotic areas, because they have not addressed the urgent problems mainstream research has been dedicated to. Even though this might be surprising, because comparative education has been a field of research since Marc-Antoine Jullien's (1775–1848) publication "Esquisse et vues préliminaires d'un ouvrage sur l'éducation comparée" in 1817,[39] international student assessments such as PISA and the standards movement have changed everything. At least since the late 1990s, comparative and international education are prominent areas of research, supporting international student assessments and the creation of standards by providing data, contributing to the development of evaluation designs, and helping identify effective strategies for poorly performing educational systems. Particularly this last aspect, in terms of educational transfer, is a strong rationale for comparative education. Regarding the meaning of educational transfer for comparative education, Robert Cowen states:

> The transfer business is the public legitimization of the field, the reason we can command scarce resources. . . . Defining and analyzing "cultural borrowing" and the terms on which it is possible becomes the intellectual agenda of the field.[40]

Educational transfer is certainly an important justification for comparative or international education. But it is not unproblematic, because it questions our understanding of national educational systems and thereby the meaning of comparative education. If we are already globalized in education and music education, because of the ubiquity of international exchange, we should reassess what the meaning of comparative education is. Jeremy Rappleye might be right when he claims that "globalization has seriously challenged the way that educational policy is compared."[41] If school systems in various countries already follow an international model and international approaches, such as Orff or Kodály, it might be time to reconsider what the meaning of comparative education is. Stephen Carney states:

> Globalization, if we take this to mean both convergence and harmonization but also rupture and disjunction, suggests that comparative work in the field of educational policy concerns itself—with the very question of comparison itself. The proposition is not a call for a refined comparative education, but for a substantially different one.[42]

This indicates that, in view of globalization, there is a need for revised approaches in comparative education and music education. Comparison being at the core of research is not sufficient anymore. A variety of methods, concepts, and goals need to be considered.

Terminological and Methodological Issues

Research in education and music education addressing global issues is usually connected with two different terms: *international* and *comparative*. While these can be defined as "twin fields," with significant similarities,[43] there are also differences. Jeff Thompson states regarding international education that "it is often associated with the related concepts of global, intercultural, multinational and multicultural education, and shares a great deal of conceptual territory with dimensions of comparative education."[44] While being closely related to comparative education, international education seems to have an emphasis on intercultural and global issues, maybe even on developing countries. Comparative education, however, is more interested in understanding what education in different countries looks like and how the international flow of ideas works. Nelly Stromquist explains:

> In general, comparative education emphasizes the understanding of the dynamics of educational change and seeks to detect patterns of change across countries. International education concentrates primarily on developing countries and endeavors to gear education to the improvement and building of nation-states.[45]

This statement seems to bring out some of the main points of both areas. However, international education could also be understood as a broader term, not being bound to comparison as main method. It seems to terminologically imply developing international mindedness and intercultural understanding that fosters "an international orientation in knowledge and attitudes and, among other initiatives, brings together students, teachers, and scholars from different nations to learn about and from each other."[46] But aside from all attempts at differentiating international and comparative education, Erwin Epstein underlines that they supplement each other.[47] This can lead to the conclusion that, in view of globalization, using both terms could be helpful to having a comprehensive perspective on global challenges.

In comparative and international education, comparison plays a controversial role because it implies a single perspective and method. While in a more general way, "comparisons are . . . the basis of all knowledge,"[48] Neville Postlethwaite describes comparison in education as "examining two or more educational entities by putting them side by side and looking for similarities or differences between or among them."[49] This certainly resonates with our most common understanding of comparison as a basic epistemological procedure, which George Bereday takes, regarding education, as meaning that "to understand others and to understand ourselves is to have in hand the two ingredients of comparison."[50] As a method, comparison is not unproblematic. It can support a tendency to oversimplify and generalize, which is a well-known problem in comparative and international education and music education.[51] Additionally, there also is the issue of what is comparable and what is not. Giovanni Satori asks, referring to the vivid example of apples and pears, "Are they comparable or not?" He concludes:

> Yes, they are comparable with respect to some of their properties, that is, the properties they share, and non-comparable with respect to the properties that they do not share. Thus, pears and apples are comparable as fruits, as things that can be eaten, as entities that grow on trees; but incomparable, for example, in their respective shapes. Making the point in general, the question always is: *comparable with respect to which properties or characteristics?*[52]

Satori makes here some important points. In education and music education, there are some aspects that cannot be compared while others are comparable, such as educational provision, methods, or approaches. Mark Bray, Bob Adamson, and Mark Mason summarize these units of comparison as places, systems, times, cultures, values, educational achievements, policies, curricula, educational organizations, ways of learning, and pedagogical innovations.[53] Some of these issues are not easy to compare—for instance, cultures, values, or innovations. However, when comparison is possible, it often has one goal: to discover successful features, strategies, or policies of an educational system so that a different country can borrow them. Thomas Popkewitz supports this notion with regard to educational transfer by pointing out that "the field of comparative education . . . is designed around developing ameliorative models for the 'transferring' of ideas and practices."[54] Gita Steiner-Khamsi even suggests that "since its inception as an academic field, comparative education has been enamored with the research on educational transfer. . . . There is no doubt that the study of transfer has helped to legitimate and sustain our field."[55] But educational transfer also challenges comparative and international education, since we are comparing not different but similar features. Because of ongoing educational transfer, many attractive music education policies, strategies, or methods might be the product of borrowing. If we are already international and related, it is problematic to use comparison as a method.

But comparative education and music education are not always focused on comparison. They can also be concerned with simply collecting and providing data about education or music education systems through single-system studies.[56] The goal is to present information about a country's education or music education system. Harold Noah states about this purpose of comparative education that "a fundamental task . . . is to collect, classify and array data about educational efforts of the nations of the world."[57] The collection of data has been important for international organizations such as United Nations Educational, Scientific, and

Cultural Organization (UNESCO) or OECD, particularly considering international student assessments and the funding of specific educational programs. Single-country studies can also be a foundation for comparative studies. But even though the studies of national education and music education systems are important, comparative and international education cannot be focused only on nation-states. In view of globalization and the blurring of borders, it might no longer be appropriate to refer to the nation-state as the sole point of reference. Rather, there can also be other categories, such as comparing different regions (e.g., two or more federal states in Germany, such as Bavaria and Brandenburg). Comparisons could concern smaller units, such as individual communities or villages, or be focused on specific topics, such as the provision of education for people with special needs in rural and metropolitan areas in France. The issue of different units of comparison in comparative education is addressed by Mark Bray and Murray Thomas in their cube model.[58] By choosing the form of a cube, they illustrate different levels of comparison. These may concern studies of world regions or individual schools or be focused on aspects of education (e.g., curriculum, teaching methods) and nonlocational demographic groups (e.g., ethnic or gender groups). Bray describes the meaning of the cube:

> Along one side were aspects of education and of society, and along another side were non-locational and demographic groups. The front of the cube then presented seven geographical/locational levels. At the top were provinces, districts, schools, classrooms and individuals. We observed that comparisons could be made at each of these levels, and that the insights gained from such comparisons would differ at each level. We noted that in some respects patterns at each level were influenced by patterns at other levels. We made a case for multilevel analysis of educational phenomena; and where resources did not permit such multilevel analysis, we suggested that researchers should at least be aware of the level at which they were operating and of the limitations imposed by focusing only on that level.[59]

The cube indicates the various opportunities for comparison. The individual researcher can make informed choices about what he or she wants to study and what not. This facilitates a more systematic approach to comparison as a method in international education and music education.

Aside from Bray's cube, which has become popular in recent years, there have been many ways of addressing issues of comparative and international education and music education. Bereday's classic study, *Comparative Method in Education*, presented in 1964 important aspects for comparative education and music education. While he values the significance of collecting data, he also insists that research must be more than just a "lifeless recounting of pedagogical facts without an attempt at analysis and comparison."[60] Bereday argues for generating hypotheses from data or using it to select a specific topic.[61] This narrows the focus down to a specific objective, such as action-oriented music education methods in Brazil and France, thereby following a problem-oriented approach. Bereday states that such a focus could lead to identifying a "typology of an educational problem," studying the same theme in different countries and thereby helping improve the educational systems.[62] For Bereday, comparative education should follow a four-step model for a successful comparative analysis: In the first stage, pedagogical data are collected. The second stage concerns the interpretation in terms of an evaluation of the pedagogical data. The third level, the juxtaposition, tries to identify similarities and differences, including creating a hypothesis for the comparative analysis. The fourth stage comprises a simultaneous comparison to test the hypothesis and to summarize the results.[63] Bereday's model provides a clear methodology for conducting successful comparative research. The most striking aspect is the emphasis on the problem-oriented approach. It is not enough to gather data and to compare. Rather, there is a need for focusing on a specific topic. I have argued in a similar way regarding comparative music education.[64] Referring to similar problems in music education worldwide, such as the implementation of standards, assessment, or multicultural music education, can be a useful way to conduct comparative or cross-cultural analysis: "An approach that is cross-cultural and focused on certain areas is far more effective than looking at a whole system of music education."[65] By scrutinizing specific issues, comparative research can be rendered much more effective than it would be by looking at an entire educational system. Anthony Kemp and Laurence Lepherd argue similarly by referring to research by Brian Holmes and George Bereday[66] and suggesting six categories as useful for single-nation or comparative analysis: the aims (child-centered, society-centered, subject-centered), administration, finance, structure and organization of music education, curricula, and teacher education. This indicates that comparative education needs a clear focus and direction to be successful.[67]

But when dealing with research in international and comparative education, it is important to know what the general purpose of this research is. Holmes states about the intentions of comparative education:

> (1) Comparative education should lead to a greater understanding of processes of education; (2) it should promote interest in and information about particular national systems of education and be able to explain why they are as they are; (3) it should facilitate the practical reform and planned development of school systems; (4) it should promote desirable international attitudes among those who study it.[68]

This indicates that comparative education not only aims at descriptions of school systems but also at educational improvement, possibly in terms of educational transfer. While information and data about educational systems are important, even providing "a political geography of schools," as Bereday explains,[69] this cannot be sufficient. Wilfried Halls elaborates that comparative education should analyze the dimensions of education, especially the relationship between society and education, and "distinguish the fundamental condition of educational change and persistence and relate these to more ultimate philosophical laws."[70] He thereby emphasizes intentions of comparative education that go beyond pure descriptions, instead aiming at understanding and uncovering the foundations of education in various countries, with a focus on the impact the society with its educational ideals has. This statement seems to evoke Bray's cube and the interconnectedness of the different levels that can be addressed by comparative education. But it also illustrates that comparative education most certainly is an interdisciplinary endeavor, depending on the expertise of related disciplines, such as sociology or policy studies.

This raises an interesting issue: Is comparative education a discipline or just a subfield of education? António Nóvoa elaborates the two perspectives on this aspect eloquently:

> It is quite easy to line up the arguments against a field which has never succeeded in defining either a proper objective or even a method, which is midway between scientific research and political intervention, . . . [and] which depend[s] rather on a certain academic folklore than a systematic production of knowledge. . . . [W]e would even go so far as to denounce the illusion of being able to build a discipline on a method, comparison, which is inherent in every scientific approach.[71]

Nóvoa makes some important points: Without a sound method and a clear purpose, comparative education could not be an independent scholarly discipline. It is situated between various fields, even between pure research and political action. Additionally, comparative education most often deals with stereotypes about national educational systems, which Nóvoa calls "folklore." These biases are certainly dangerous territory for a scholarly field and need to be challenged constantly. However, there are also arguments in favor of comparative education being a discipline. Nóvoa continues:

> It is also easy to praise a field which looks for explanation beyond national limits, which calls on multi-disciplinary approaches, which does not hesitate to come to terms with the inevitable links between educational research and educational action; the plea in favour could go so far as to assert that comparative education is the quintessence of the educational sciences, since it is situated at . . . "a higher epistemological level."[72]

Some of the aspects that have been weaknesses in the description before are now turned into strengths: comparative education goes beyond the limits of common disciplines. It is on another epistemological level, dealing with the rules and foundations of what educational research is. Therefore, there is no need to fit any kind of narrow definition. Being an interdisciplinary endeavor, not being restricted to the limits of a single field, can be an advantage. Rolland Paulston explains that he was fascinated by exactly this openness of comparative education, which for him is "a synthetic field" that offers him "the freedom . . . to create, to work with [his] ideas and with other people's ideas."[73] This emphasizes the significance of individual experiences, which are often marginalized in comparative and international education and music education research.

Individual Experiences

While many studies in comparative and international education are focused on aspects such as the provision of education, music education approaches, or teacher education programs, researchers' individual experiences are often overlooked. This is particularly surprising since living in a foreign country is often an indispensable requirement for comparative or international research, including processes of socialization or enculturation. Bereday even argues that traveling, spending time in a different country, and becoming familiar with it are necessary to conduct effective comparative research in education.[74]

However, in recent years, at least, a few researchers have emphasized the need for the "subjectivity of comparative research," arguing for a variety of research methods, including ethnographic ones, and also stories or autobiographical writing.[75] This new approach is certainly part of a general transformation in comparative and international education, realizing the social relatedness of studies in this field. Regarding the value of personal experiences for comparative education, Patricia Potts asserts:

> In the context of education, the devaluation of learning from experience seems particularly wasteful. Social knowledge is dynamic, unstable and contingent, but this reduces neither its scope nor its value.[76]

Potts raises an important issue: we need to acknowledge the meaning of personal experiences, particularly regarding education, which is to a certain degree based on personal relationships. In view of poststructuralist notions emphasizing that the objectivity of research is only an illusion, it might be time to acknowledge the individual voices of researchers in comparative education even more. This will open new insights.

The researcher's experiences in a foreign country and its music education system play a major role for studies in international and comparative education. It would most likely make a difference regarding the research results if somebody spent a decade in a country or visited it only briefly. Phillips and Schweisfurth illustrate these aspects that affect the complicated relationship between the researcher and the researched in comparative and international (music) education with a continuum showing that every researcher finds herself traveling between extremes, such as familiar or unfamiliar, similar or different to home culture, viewed with a monocultural or comparative perspective, and interculturally skilled or unskilled.[77] A researcher's new context can be familiar or unfamiliar, depending on the time spent in a country, a city, or a region but also on the amount of the researcher's reflectiveness, his or her language skills, or the need for direct contact with schools or people.

In my own experience as a postdoctoral researcher at the University of Washington in Seattle, from 2002 until 2005, I found that much was unfamiliar at the beginning: the language, the way of living, the music education, and the university system. Over time, I became familiar with these aspects, starting with music education vocabulary, the system of music education in schools, and the way seminars and universities work. This was often a challenging process, and I had to go through different stages along the continuum from unfamiliar to familiar. Some of my experiences were certainly like the ones described in culture shock theories and the related phases, such as the honeymoon phase, crisis, relaxation, and adaptation.[78] A kind of socialization had to take place, which was supported by significant people as well as my self-reflection. Another crucial aspect of the researcher's perspective is the new environment's similarity to or difference from the researcher's home culture. This can concern the language, the political system, gender relationships, or family structures. For a researcher investigating a new music education system, it is important to realize deliberately these similarities and differences. This means making explicit the sometimes unconscious process of comparing everything one encounters with the home culture. For me, as a postdoctoral researcher in the United States, this meant discerning that even though many aspects of American music education seemed to be different (e.g., buildings, terminology, performance-based music education), there were many commonalities with German music education, due to educational transfer. The overall feeling of strangeness, however, because I was unfamiliar with so many things, made it difficult for me to notice the commonalities. It took a deliberate effort to go beyond this initial feeling of strangeness to consciously realize what was familiar and unfamiliar. Over time, my perspective changed and, in the end, American music education seemed in many respects much more familiar to me than German music education. Consciously experiencing this process from unfamiliarity to familiarity was interesting and certainly helped me develop a bicultural perspective, overcoming my originally rather monocultural point of view, defining everything in relation to German music education.

However, no matter how much time a researcher spends in another country, he or she can continue to hold on to a monocultural perspective and an ethnocentric attitude. This can include assuming the implicit superiority of one culture—for instance, as related to cultural values such as democracy or women's rights. For me, this meant not falling into the trap of assuming that, for example, the German educational tradition of *Bildung*, with its emphasis on formation and educating self-determined and mature human beings, might be superior to maybe superficial American educational ideals. This also concerned the German approach of general music education, fostering various musical abilities. While I noticed that, particularly in American high schools, bands and orchestras were often far more advanced than German school ensembles, it took me some time to realize the respective intentions and values of each music education system without assuming that one or the other was superior. This also concerns developing intercultural skills and competencies by critically reflecting on one's own culture, being curious about other cultures, speaking other languages, or using analytical awareness to help overcome bias.[79] These abilities and perspectives are part of the continuum a researcher in comparative education and music education passes through.[80] The continuum characterizes the transformation an individual researcher might experience. Reflectiveness plays a significant role in this endeavor, underlining that this process does not happen automatically but needs refinement and individual engagement.

In Chris Harrison and Sarah Hennessy's *Listen Out: International Perspectives on Music Education*, the reports of music students and music teachers studying and working abroad illustrate experiences to be had in foreign countries and their individual value.[81] But even though some of the reports describe the experiences of a German exchange student in the United Kingdom,[82] music teaching in contexts such as Japan or England,[83] or young people's experiences of music learning in different countries,[84] it is important to connect these sometimes very personal experiences with scholarly theories and concepts within the realm of comparative and international music education. Relating individual experiences to adequate research frameworks and methodologies helps make the best out of them. Then, individual voices at various career stages can be valuable for comparative and international music education and truly foster the formation of the international music education community.

Considering comparative and international music education as foundation for music education research worldwide is an important part of globalizing music education. Therefore, this is a significant conceptual element of a framework for facilitating the development of a united and diverse global music education community. This leads to the question of what constitutes such a community and how its formation can be nurtured.

Global Community

Globalization underlines that our futures worldwide are connected. As music educators, we are part of the global music education community. This certainly raises some questions: What kind of community are we? What unites and differentiates us? Who might not be part of this community and why? It is crucial to consider these challenges to find ways to foster the further development of the global community in a way acknowledging the diversity of music education and research cultures worldwide. This is what globalizing music education means.

Global Perspectives

The daily work of music educators is similar worldwide, despite national or regional differences. Most basically, this work is about people and music. Marie McCarthy states that, internationally, music educators "are united by a common purpose: to engage children and youth in music and to develop their artistic life and their humanity."[85] Music educators facilitate people's musical activities and learning processes, thereby offering opportunities for personal transformations. Around the globe, they face similar challenges in their daily lives and have to come to terms with multifarious roles as identified by research in sociology of music education: music educators are certainly citizens of the world and feel responsible for the planet's future; they are musicians and music(k)ers, whether professionals or amateurs, and celebrate their passion for music through their actions; as music experts, conductors, educational professionals, scholars, administrators, or politicians, they actualize music through musical engagement and advocate its benefits; as employees in schools, universities, community music schools, or other workplaces, they put their pedagogical and musical beliefs into practice; and as leaders and coleaders, they are in charge of music and music education, trying to be lifelong learners, working toward a better world, equal opportunities, and social justice.[86] These and many more roles are part of the daily work of music educators worldwide. However, some music educators might struggle with balancing some of these roles—for example, musician and teacher. Other musicians or educators might not be able to identify at all with any of the roles mentioned.

Aside from these roles and conflicts, music educators working in schools worldwide face professional challenges that are related to music education as part of the school curriculum. McCarthy identifies six issues: (1) the status of music education, (2) music education advocacy, (3) curriculum development and reform, (4) whose music is presented in the curriculum, (5) the changing culture of pedagogy, and (6) professional networks.[87] Some of these aspects might be more prominent than others in each country, depending on the political, economic, and cultural situation or the history of music education. Particularly the historical development of music education in a country is interesting, because there are global commonalities.[88] Often, patriotic or religious notions were the main reasons for introducing music education in public schools, as was the case in Germany at the beginning of the nineteenth century.[89] Educating loyal citizens and fostering religious feelings through choral singing within the school community were the most common justifications for music as part of the public school curriculum.

While, over time, many more rationales for music education worldwide have emerged, whether promoting health and well-being through singing, nurturing the formation of the personality, or fostering intelligence and creativity, the connection between music education and patriotism has always been a strong one.[90] This origin of music education in public schools is certainly something that unites music educators worldwide and is part of the heritage of the global music education profession, in some countries more obviously than in others.

However, even though the beginning of music education in public schools was similar, today many differences can be observed. This concerns music education in schools being either a mandatory or an elective subject, and maybe even an extracurricular activity. The favored music education approach might also vary: in countries such as Ireland or Germany it is general music education, while in others, such as the United States, performance-based music education is the most common approach, particularly in secondary schools. Methods such as Orff, Kodály, or Dalcroze are internationally popular but transformed according to the specific needs of a national music education system. In many countries worldwide, particularly in the economically more developed countries, technology and digital media play an important role in music education.[91] They facilitate music making or learning and relate it to popular culture and the musical worlds of young people. Often, music education is connected to the national, regional, or local music culture. But it is also possible that the national music culture is marginalized in music education in public schools in favor of classical music, as has happened in Japan.[92]

It is important to notice these commonalities and differences in music education around the globe. But we also need to consider that more than one perspective should be the main point of reference, not just, for instance, the Western European or Anglo-American one. McCarthy is correct when she states that "international perspectives in music education are founded on and dominated by narratives from Western countries and those influenced by the colonial presence of European countries."[93] Too often, international music education is concentrated on discourses initiated and dominated by scholars from Anglo-American or European countries. Many voices and narratives from different parts of the world are marginalized. In view of the need for globalizing music education, it is time to raise awareness of this tendency and to try to include the voices of music educators and scholars from various countries in the international discourse. This will help us become the diverse global community we need to be to master the challenges ahead.

Community or Profession?

As mentioned above, there are different perspectives on what unites us as a global music education community. One of them is certainly related to professionalism, in terms of defining music education as a distinct profession. If music education is thought to be a profession, it might have the following characteristics:

> (a) A distinct body of technical knowledge; (b) a certain level of commitment, from the part of [its] members, to the professional norms of practice; (c) an association or peer group that aims at regulating the entry into practice and controls the professional practice and its transformation; (d) monopoly of the practice—that is to say, that the group has successfully acquired or secured its dominance over its respective practice. This monopoly is, in fact, confirmed by the state, who supports and secures [it] by law.[94]

This description addresses different levels of a profession, such as knowledge and skills, norms, gatekeeper functions, and recognition by the state. It approaches, in a rather technical way, what characterizes a craft or trade as something for which an education, training, or apprenticeship is a requirement. This constitutes an exclusiveness of the profession, as only those who have successfully finished their education can work and earn their living in the respective field. These characteristics of a profession can easily be applied to music education: professional musicians need to have a specific domain knowledge and related competencies; commitment and submitting to specific norms is also part of being a musician or teacher; and certainly, there are degree-granting institutions, such as conservatories or schools of music regulating access to education and the job market, transmitting and transforming current practices and values. In some fields, such as music education in public schools, there is also the "monopoly over practice": without proper licensing, no access to the occupation of music teacher in public schools is granted in many countries. However, these aspects would certainly not apply to music instruction in general, because there are several ways of becoming a musician or teacher, particularly in different cultures. Applying this rather narrow definition as presented by Jonathan Parquette would mean withholding the status of professional musician or educator from many musicians worldwide—for example, in the realm of jazz, popular music, or music of various cultures. There are many ways of becoming a musician, a music teacher, or an educator. Some paths might lead through degree-granting institutions, others might not. In view of the global music education community, it is important to consider the role professionalism plays, but it is also crucial to know the limits this concept has.

Wayne Bowman therefore critically questions the notion of music education as a profession. For him, there is the danger that professionalism in music education leads to elitism and exclusiveness if professions contain "self-defined elites" who earn this status through acquiring specific knowledge and skills requiring intense study.[95] This would exclude many people from the music education profession who are not able to gain this proficiency, resulting in a clear distinction between professionals and amateurs, differentiating the "we" from the "other."

Bowman is particularly concerned about the musicianship of the people who are excluded.[96] He fears that a kind of musicianship related to classical music that has long been promoted by conservatories and schools of music would determine who is part of the music education profession. In so doing, the diversity of musical practices and the social embeddedness of music might be excluded from the common definition of professionalism. While it is certainly right that the definition of music determines what music education and professionalism is, the related fears might be outdated. Popular music and the music of various cultures of the world have been part of the curriculum in the conservatories and schools of music worldwide for some decades now, broadening and supplementing the understanding of musical professionalism, also that of music education. There is no danger that these musical practices can be excluded from the music or the music education profession. However, for Bowman, the only way to guarantee diversity in music education, with respect to the musical and cultural background of people entering the profession, is an open understanding of professionalism:

> How diverse and pluralistic music education is, or can be, is a direct function of the diversity and pluralism of our membership, our musical practices, and their attendant curricula. Is the voice of music education the voice of heterodoxy or is it the voice of orthodoxy? Is it the voice of progress or the voice of suppression?[97]

There are certainly some important points here. But the assumption that professionalism could equal exclusivity and orthodox musical paradigms as related to classical music seems to be outdated.

In general, there is nothing wrong with professionals being part of the global music education community. But there are also other groups within this community. Being part of a profession does not have to be exclusive but rather differentiates a certain group of people from others, characterizing their specific duties and functions. Our daily work environment relies on the differentiation in professionals, semiprofessionals, and nonprofessionals. Most of us highly appreciate this and rather more trust a physician or a carpenter when they are professionals. While the analogy of physician and musician might not be appropriate in all regards, it points out some significant aspects: preferring professionals or nonprofessionals depends on the situation and the expectations one has. That professionals in music or music education exist does not mean that we might always prefer them to nonprofessionals. A concert played by an amateur orchestra might sometimes be more exciting than a concert played by a professional orchestra. Nonprofessional musicians can have a kind of motivation and passion that professionals sometimes do not always have anymore. Differentiating between members and nonmembers of a profession is not, then, discriminatory but rather exemplifies different ways of approaching being a musician or a music educator. Bowman's question "How do we pursue greater diversity without compromising professional standards?" thus does not present the only two alternatives.[98] There are various ways of being a musician and a music educator that do not depend on degrees or proficiency. There are some parts of the music and music education work world where experts are needed. But whether professional, semiprofessional, amateur, or somebody between all categories, our passion for people and music unites us as a global music education community.

However, Bowman might not have international music education in mind, even though the greater part of his paper is devoted to the discussion of music education and professionalism in general. Rather, he is particularly concerned with music education in North America. When he examines gatekeeping practices, he states, "Entrance and graduation requirements in North American undergraduate programs assure that only people like 'us' (White? Middle class? Able? Politely compliant?) enter the field."[99] This indicates that he derives the main points of his argument from the situation in North America without explicitly stating so at the beginning. This is an interesting example of an unconscious focus on Anglo-American or North American music education practices without even questioning whether the research results are generally applicable. In this regard, Bowman's paper is certainly no exception. Many publications imply that they deal with music education in general, but are, in fact, focused on Anglo-American music education. There needs to be more critical awareness of this practice. It would be useful if authors writing from a certain perspective would point this out. However, despite all issues related to the hidden hegemony of Anglo-American music education, Bowman's main point of embracing diversity within the music education profession, maybe having "more porous borders, a more inclusive 'we,'"[100] is important in view of globalization and internationalization.

Apart from seeing the global music education community from the perspective of professionalism, it can also be understood as a symbolic community. It is characterized by shared practices, beliefs, and values. These commonalities result in a sense of belonging to such a symbolic community.[101] Identity formation plays a major role in the symbolic community and takes place in contexts that could be a university's music education program or at regional, national, or international conferences or elsewhere. Studying research journals, exchanging ideas with colleagues, or being part of a local network of music educators also strengthens the sense of belonging to a symbolic community. With today's communication technology, a sense of belonging can be established beyond the borders of countries or regions. A symbolic community does not need to be a geopolitical community, and diversity is welcome. Hildegard Froehlich asserts, "Diversity can be shared and celebrated best if a sense of belonging has been established."[102] Being united by a basic set of beliefs is sufficient to be a member of a symbolic community. Differences are not obstacles to membership in a symbolic community but rather enrich it. It is, however, the task of music educators to "work toward a sense of belonging across various geographical locales and for diverse social networks and groups."[103]

This indicates that the global music education community is a work in progress. Fostering a sense of unity while valuing diversity certainly involves transformative processes for individuals and the community. This is an indispensable condition for becoming a global music education community. While the notion of symbolic community certainly provides an excellent concept for what we are or could be, the concept of "imagined community," as developed by Benedict Anderson regarding nations and their respective ideas of unity, might also be useful. "Imagined" means for Anderson that "the members of even the smallest nation will never know most of their fellow-members, meet them, or even hear of them, yet in the minds of each lives the images of their communion."[104] This understanding of imagined community emphasizes that it does not matter that the members of a community will never have a chance to get to know each other. They can still be connected through shared values and beliefs. The global music education community might be an imagined community.

In the end, it does not matter whether the global music education community is a symbolic or an imagined community. The sense of shared values and beliefs and the richness of diversity give a sense of identity and empower its members. It might be an important task for music education programs in universities and for organizations concerned with facilitating musical activities internationally, such as International Society for Music Education (ISME), to foster this sense of belonging to a global community. But individual members also have the opportunity and even the duty to shape globalizing music education in a way that acknowledges the dialectics of unity and diversity, both in their daily lives and on institutional levels, in music education policy or advocacy. It is important to know that we are not alone in our daily struggles and victories as music educators and scholars.

Scholarly Cultures

When talking about international commonalities and differences, it is also crucial to look at scholarly cultures in music education worldwide. While the differences in music education among countries are obvious and have been addressed by comparative and cross-cultural research, the characteristics of music education as a field of research in different countries are often overlooked, particularly in view of the international hegemony of Anglo-American music education.

Music education as a distinct field of research differentiates itself from neighboring fields such as education or musicology. It has its own history, methods, goals, discourses, and scholarly culture. It is a scholarly discipline. A discipline is, as Ken Hyland states, "a common label used to describe and distinguish topics, knowledge, institutional structures and individuals in the world of scholarship."[105] Disciplines offer scholars a community to belong to. They give them an identity as researchers in a specific field. Tony Becher describes the characteristics of disciplinary communities as specific "traditions, customs and practices, transmitted knowledge, beliefs, morals and rules of conduct, as well as their linguistic and symbolic forms of communication and the meanings they share."[106] These features can easily be applied to music education. There certainly is domain-specific knowledge of music learning and teaching. There are related beliefs, traditions, and common practices of thinking and acting. There are specific concepts, theories, and approaches that many people in music education internationally know and use—for example, basic principles of the Orff approach. To be admitted to this community, a certain amount of knowledge and skills is necessary. However, "not only a sufficient level of technical proficiency in one's intellectual trade but also a proper measure of loyalty to one's collegial group and of adherence to its norms" is important, as Becher states.[107] Scholarly communities follow certain rules and expect new members to become familiar with them, as well as with scholarly authorities and their theories. Knowledge about important publications and scholars in a field such as music education is essential. Burton Clark asserts ironically, "The culture of a discipline includes idols: the pictures on the walls and dustjackets of books kept in view are of Albert Einstein and Max Planck and Robert Oppenheimer in the office of the physicist and of Max Weber and Karl Marx and Emil Durkheim in the office of the sociologist."[108] There are also scholarly "heroes" in the world of music education, their books being on shelves in music education offices worldwide. But the variety of scholarly interests and the membership in specific research groups within the scholarly community of music education—for example, philosophy or sociology of music education—might result in different classic publications on the book shelves. While there are national scholarly cultures in music education as well, resulting in specific scholarly authorities and important publications in a country, an international disciplinary identity with significant global figures and publications has emerged.[109] Estelle Jorgensen's *Transforming Music Education*,[110] David Elliott's *Music Matters*,[111] and Patricia Shehan Campbell's *Songs in Their Heads*[112] are important points of reference in international music education. Handbooks such as Gary McPherson and Graham Welch's *Oxford Handbook of Music Education* also play significant roles in the formation of the global scholarly community.[113]

Furthermore, specific fields of research, such as philosophy of music education, have fostered the formation of the global music education community significantly, through publications in, for example, the *Philosophy of Music Education Review*,[114] which supports the discourse about international issues, organizes international conferences, and has established the International Society for the Philosophy of Music Education.[115] This underlines that there are various ways of supporting the formation of an international music education community and globalizing music education, whether from the perspective of profession or scholarly community. We are all part of this process and can have an impact on it. Therefore, positing the notion of global community as a conceptual element in a framework facilitating globalizing music education in a culturally sensitive way is important. It supports creating a broader vision of the global music education and research profession. Another important conceptual element contributing to this vision is global knowledge production.

Global Knowledge Production

Research and publishing are part of the work of scholars worldwide. Globalization and internationalization have created a global scholarly community and knowledge market. Geographical, geolinguistic, geopolitical, and other factors have an impact on the production of knowledge. The country and the institution where a scholar works, the language she or he writes in, and the policies regarding research and its evaluation play significant roles in global knowledge production.[116] It is important to raise awareness for some of the challenges music education scholars are facing in a global world. Therefore, global knowledge production is a significant element in a conceptual framework facilitating globalizing music education.

Global and Local Knowledge

In a globalized world, knowledge production in terms of research and publishing serves the improvement of music education worldwide. Scholars and music educators around the world make significant contributions, publish books or articles, give presentations, and prepare their students for a diverse music education world. They produce local or global knowledge, either related to the country they work in and its respective scholarly community or concerned with global issues, aiming at an international audience. While to a certain degree all knowledge might be local in terms of originating within a specific sociocultural context—for example, the French music education system—there is a general tendency to be particularly interested in global knowledge as being useful for the global music education community. This interest in universal knowledge is part of our general notion of research and higher education. Particularly the Enlightenment and its epistemology had an impact on these notions, thereby turning originally local knowledge as situated in Western Europe in the seventeenth and eighteenth centuries, related to specific sociocultural conditions, into a global concept. Ken Hyland might be right when stating that the Enlightenment was "the most successful transformation of local knowledge into global."[117] Stuart Hall underlines this assumption by pointing out that the global perspective is to a certain degree just the way a dominant culture might orchestrate itself, using possibly objectified reasons to justify its hegemony.[118] This illustrates that our understanding of knowledge and science is not universal but rather derived from concepts developed at a certain time and in a specific part of the world. While this is certainly a well-known fact and philosophical research has extensively addressed this issue,[119] this realization can open new perspectives on music education research. We need to consider more critically what is thought to be global knowledge. It might, in fact, be only the knowledge one music education tradition, such as the Anglo-American one, thinks important, thereby marginalizing the meaning of local or national knowledge—for example, from Latin America—for the global music education community. But the voices of researchers and teachers from various music education cultures are important to improve music education worldwide.

There is a need for an open discourse about what kind of knowledge we consider to be important for the global music education community. While there will certainly always be knowledge as related to specific nations or regions, published in respective scholarly journals, possibly written in the native language of the interested audience, it is no easy task to decide what knowledge is of universal interest. Hyland underlines this problem when stating that "knowledge must emerge from a particular locality, but it is then published and added to either a local or a global stock of knowledge."[120] We need to acknowledge the diversity of music education and research perspectives and overcome preconceptions regarding research from specific parts of the world, no matter if from a remote part of Asia or from Western Europe. The locality should not be the major reason why we exclude certain kinds of research from our global stock of knowledge. There needs to be more awareness for the role geographical, geolinguistic, or geopolitical factors play in the generation of global knowledge.

This concerns not only publications but also university programs. Many scholars from different countries are trained at Western universities. They often must give up a part of their local or national identity as music educators to fit into and function in a foreign university system. In view of globalization and the global mobility of students and scholars, we need to recognize the meaning of the diverse music education and research cultures many students and scholars are socialized in. They offer much-needed new perspectives on music education and could contribute significantly to globalizing music education. Regarding the marginalization of local knowledge at universities, Athelstan Canagarajah states correctly that "what is left out is the local knowledge that constitutes the perspectives and practices of the disempowered."[121] We need to acknowledge the many kinds of knowledge and help international students and scholars overcome their feeling of powerlessness and the marginalization of their music education experiences. While universities certainly aim at generating and teaching universal knowledge, there should be room for integrating local and national traditions, thereby helping international students feel empowered and use their local and national knowledge to foster and shape globalizing music education in a culturally sensitive way. Issues of language play a significant role in this process.

Language and Terminology

While English as an academic language facilitates international communication in music education, it also fosters a dangerous illusion—namely, that literal translations are possible and that there is no difference between a foreign term and its English equivalent. However, sociolinguistic research indicates that the meaning of words changes through translations.[122] This is even more critical in specialized areas of language such as music education terminology. There is a great variety of music education systems worldwide, many of them relying on unique terminology. Often, the meaning of significant terms cannot be translated, only approximated. The German terms *Didaktik* and *Bildung* are examples. *Didaktik* describes the science and art of teaching, concerning both theory and practice. It is at the core of German teacher education programs and training. It enables music teachers to be self-determined educational professionals who can make informed pedagogical decisions regarding, for example, lesson content or structure, on the basis of common models of music teaching and learning. This understanding of *Didaktik* is certainly different from the English term *didactic*, which might be thought to be an adequate translation because of having the same word root. But in fact, the English *didactic* mostly describes an authoritarian teaching style and is not at all related to the student-centered and action-oriented approach the German *Didaktik* stands for.[123] This indicates that one needs to be careful with translations, even if the terms in two languages sound similar. This also concerns *Bildung*, a pedagogical notion closely related to *Didaktik*. Even though the English terms *cultivation* and *formation* are similar, they are not able to capture *Bildung*'s meaning entirely. *Bildung* as the core idea in the history of German education describes the goal of educating self-determined, mature, and knowledgeable citizens. *Bildung* aims both at knowledge in certain subject areas, such as literature or music, and at personal development. In German music education, the notion of *Bildung* as *aesthetische Bildung* (aesthetic education) is closely linked to the concept of *aesthetische Erfahrung* (aesthetic experience), supporting important processes of personal transformation. This rudimentary description of what *Bildung* is in German education and music education clearly underlines the problems of translation. There is a need for wordy paraphrases to approach the meaning of one word. In many languages, there are terms that carry the burden of a long history and of huge educational expectations—for example, the African notion of *ubuntu*.[124] International research in education and music education should consider the limits of translation, as well as the richness of music education terms from other traditions as being able to make significant contributions to the international discourse.

Furthermore, the English translation of the German term *aesthetische Bildung*, literally "aesthetic education," exemplifies another challenge: the history of a term. In German music education, *aesthetische Bildung* is a well-known term representing a highly appreciated concept, describing an action-oriented and student-centered approach. But the Anglo-American term *aesthetic education* carries the burden of the Reimer-Elliott debate about either an education of feelings through listening or a praxial music education, supporting the personal and musical development of individuals.[125] This debate strains the term *aesthetic education* in the Anglo-American music education world and makes it almost impossible to use in a neutral way or function as a translation of *aesthetische Bildung*. This problem of translation is well known in European research but rarely in Anglo-American music education.[126] It indicates that translations can lead to confusion if the history of a term in another language is not considered. But it also shows the need for comparative and cross-cultural research on music education terminology and concepts.

This leads to the interesting question of how we should deal with national terminology in view of globalizing music education. Should we eliminate German, French, or Spanish terminology and replace it with international Anglo-American terminology? This would certainly facilitate international communication, and to some degree it is what is already going on in international music education. But it is essential to point out the value of having music education traditions from around the world. We appreciate music of different cultures and teach them in music classrooms, but we tend to ignore the richness of various music education and research cultures worldwide. It might be time to acknowledge the global diversity in music education, also embracing important terms from many countries. Globalizing music education should not lead to the elimination or marginalization of national terminology but rather be a way of introducing terms from multiple traditions and languages into the international music education terminology. Then it would really be a global music education terminology, not only an Anglo-American terminology. Using terms from other languages, even though English might still be the main academic language, would enrich music education internationally and help foster globalizing music education in a culturally sensitive way. This could be a first step toward acknowledging the diversity of scholarly cultures in music education and academic writing.[127]

Cultural Differences in Academic Writing

Scholars who publish in a foreign language face problems not only with grammar or lexis but also with rhetorical practices in terms of the presentation of arguments and the line of thought.[128] Rhetorical practices vary across cultures.

Robert Kaplan states correctly that "rhetoric . . . is not universal . . . but varies from culture to culture and even from time to time within a given culture."[129] English native speakers and scholars who are not familiar with this fact might confuse different rhetorical choices with the inability to think or write logically. This can become a significant issue for reviewers in scholarly journals. However, when writing in a foreign language, it is not easy to change rhetorical strategies: "Native rhetoric is so fundamental to a writer's internationalized beliefs about writing that it is difficult to change without deliberate effort and awareness of differences."[130] It is important to notice that each writer is socialized into a specific writing culture and the rhetorical practices of his or her native language. It is crucial that music education scholars and reviewers—particularly Anglo-American ones—take this into account. In view of globalization, the familiarity with the diversity of scholarly writing cultures in music education is important and can help change review practices of journals.

These differences in scholarly writing are also exemplified by publications in German and American philosophy of music education. Even though philosophy of music education in the United States and Germany might not seem so different—for example, regarding research questions or methods—they nevertheless differ in some aspects.[131] German research in philosophy of music education can, for international or Anglo-American readers, sometimes seem rather abstract and academic, rarely related to individual experiences or music education classrooms. It is not so much concerned with developing innovative ideas as with referring to scholarly authorities and defining terms. The ideal of scientific objectivity is important. Presenting results of research is at the core and not so much describing extensively the considerations that eventually lead to certain propositions. However, from a German perspective, the Anglo-American philosophy of music education values the freedom of thinking and is sometimes not so much focused on systematic analysis. Rather, it sounds to German ears like free improvisations on a given theme. To create their own perspective on a topic, authors often combine philosophical sources. Creativity and individual experiences are important points of reference to actually philosophize and not only talk about it. In general, the differences between the German and the American philosophy of music education might be the result of two concepts in higher education, the British model of discussing, considering, and relating ideas to one's own experiences and the German model of objective scientific reflection, in which the perspectives of scholarly authorities are much more important than the individual researcher's opinions. Even though the American university is a combination of the German and British higher education culture, it seems that the British influence still dominates some parts of American music education research.[132]

These observations on different scholarly traditions are backed up by research in sociolinguistics. German scholar Winfried Thielmann has analyzed the organization of German and English scholarly papers in various fields and identified significantly different rhetoric traditions and scholarly practices.[133] For introductions, for example, he found that German papers are written for experts, while the English articles do not rely so much on readers' previous knowledge and therefore explain many things.[134] German authors, however, expect readers to know a lot. The focus of articles is a rather specific perspective on a certain topic, how an author interprets facts, and how the author's opinion differs from possible other positions. Defining significant terms in the specific way the author understands them is therefore an important task. Because the German author expects her reader to have expert knowledge, there is no need to explain everything. Additionally, the reader trusts the author and does not need any kind of elaborate rhetorical strategies to become convinced. In English articles, the author explicitly tries to persuade the reader and does not just deliver information. He or she prefers a rather linear and logical line of thought, because she wants the reader to follow her. Introductions and sometimes complete papers seem to be organized like a conversation, not always focused on facts but rather following a more discursive style. Often, to convince the reader, the author does not follow the shortest route to present the facts but prefers detours via specific rhetorical strategies that help in persuading the reader of the truth of the argument.

These general differences between German and English papers support the impression that, to German readers, for example, English articles in philosophy of music education seem sometimes rather superficial and entertaining, while German papers appear to American scholars occasionally to be abstract and useless, mainly concerned with defining important terms. These observations are supported by additional findings about linguistic details: The use of the conjunctions *weil* in German and its English counterpart *because* is different, *because* appearing twice as often in English papers as the German *weil*. While *because* supports convincing the reader of the author's opinion, the German *weil* rather serves to refer to former knowledge, both in general and regarding the author's argument.[135] Additionally, the frequent use of deverbal nouns in English papers supports the impression of a certain dynamic and development.

In view of these and many more differences between German and English scholarly papers, Thielmann argues against literal translations of papers. To meet their readers' needs and the expectations of an international audience, a reorganization of papers according to the respective writing culture can be useful. But this also includes scholars becoming familiar with different writing cultures. Thielmann thus argues for an initiation into different rhetorical practices. This socialization in terms of becoming familiar with a distinct writing style and way of organizing an argument could help students and scholars be more successful regarding peer review in international journals. Nevertheless, international scholars should certainly not completely abandon their own writing style and research tradition. Being familiar with international standards of scholarly writing is a significant accomplishment in a global world. However, it is important to raise awareness for cultural differences in rhetorical practices and the role language plays in the review process in international music education.

The Power of Gatekeepers

Reviewers work as gatekeepers. They make decisions about what new knowledge would be a valuable contribution to the field. But originality is not the only criterion, because new knowledge needs to be situated within the wider framework of a scholarly field. Hyland underlines that originality in research is not "the expression of an autonomous self, but of writing that is rooted in and builds on the existing theories, discourses, and topics already legitimated in the community."[136] Balancing the tension between originality and the connection to the approved knowledge of a discipline is sometimes not an easy task for reviewers.

Reviewers make sure that publications meet scholarly standards. But these standards are not something the international music education community has purposefully agreed on but rather derived mostly from practices in Anglo-American research and standards of good English.[137] Theresa Lillis and Mary Jane Curry are certainly right when they state that "academic text production globally is powerfully shaped by the privileged status of English as the medium of publication as well as, increasingly, its codification into systems of evaluation."[138] It is certainly problematic that Anglo-American standards of scholarly writing are guidelines for peer review in international journals. It might marginalize the research of scholars not sufficiently familiar with these standards. Furthermore, many scholars and editors do not realize that the way they review and evaluate texts is determined by Anglo-American standards. Anna Mauranen and her colleagues state:

> In absence of clear standards of text organization, it has been easy to make a leap in the thought chain and assume that if English is the language of scientific publication, we should not only observe basic grammatical rules of correctness of Standard English, but follow the Anglo-American lead in matters of stylistic and rhetorical preferences as well.[139]

This statement underlines that the adoption of English as the global language in many fields in higher education has led to the impression that not only should lexicogrammatical errors be avoided but also the text organization should fit Anglo-American notions of good writing. This has an impact on the review process and favors papers from authors familiar with the Anglo-American writing culture. It puts scholars outside the Anglo-American music education world at a disadvantage. They face rejection and comments from reviewers that are not focused so much on the value of their research but rather on their language abilities and rhetorical choices. Reviewers sometimes tend to question the general value of research on the basis of language capacity. Lillis and Curry illustrate this by presenting reviewers' comments about scholarly papers from Spanish authors:

> These papers do not want reading, they want translation. Poor writing doesn't encourage the reader to turn the page. . . . The comment is not about the authors' competence in scientific English. It is about thinking.[140]

This statement indicates that the reviewer is not able to distinguish between linguistic problems or the different rhetorical choices of a nonnative English speaker and general scholarly abilities. Clarity of linguistic expression is confused with clarity of thinking and scholarly competencies. If the author is not able to express the main points of her research according to the Anglo-American standards of good writing, then this might lead to a mistaken assumption that the value of the research in general is in question. Scholarly ability and the general value of research should not be confused with lexicogrammatical mistakes or unfamiliar rhetorical choices. What is needed are more objective reviews, focused on scholarly papers' real issues, and also more awareness of the problems an international scholar encounters. The following reviewer's comment supports this need, even though it is a little bit more sympathetic:

> Unfortunately, the writing is still unclear and difficult to follow in many sections of the manuscript. I truly sympathize with you because I suspect that English may be a second language. However, the lack of clarity and jumps in logic make it hard for the reader to understand the basic message. . . . Below are a few suggestions that you might consider. I do not mean to be disrespectful by providing extremely specific comments. I realize that this is your paper and the words need to be your own. I only offer these suggestions to make the manuscript easier for the readers to understand.[141]

This statement raises other issues with which scholars whose native language is not English are familiar. The reviewer suggests words and phrases that could replace the possibly confusing language of the author, who is a nonnative English speaker. The reviewer thereby patronizes the author and puts himself into a position of authority and power, implying that he might know better what the author wants to say. This hegemony of the native speaker marginalizing the author's own linguistic and scholarly abilities is critical. While it can be useful to offer suggestions for linguistic revisions, there should also be the possibility of using different rhetorical practices. The international diversity of scholarly practices in music education exists, and it is time to acknowledge this in international publications.

Another interesting example, raising new questions, is the following comment by a reviewer:

The style needs to be polished. In any instance sentences follow each other without logical connections and the *authors often refer to other publications that may not be available to the ordinary unilingual or even bilingual North American reader.*[142]

This statement underlines that reviewers often have the Anglo-American or even North American reader in mind. Therefore, authors should only refer to English-language research that is accessible for the usual reader who might not have sufficient knowledge of foreign languages. However, when writing for an international audience, referring to international research should not be a reason for critique. While it is certainly important to have some references to research published in English, publications in other languages should certainly be welcome, too. In view of the global music education community, it is even desirable that authors refer to research in other languages, broadening the scholarly horizon of monolingual readers, thereby maybe motivating them to expand their knowledge of foreign languages or to carefully use web-based translation services. National discourses need to be related to international discourses. This will foster globalizing music education in a way acknowledging the diversity of music education research worldwide.

In general, it is important to raise awareness for the hidden hegemony of Anglo-American research and English as a global language in international music education. Critically discussing the impact this has would be a first step toward acknowledging the diversity of music education and research cultures worldwide. Lillis and Curry are right when they state that there is a "need to decentre Anglophone-centre control and to reimagine the kind of knowledge production, evaluation and distribution practices currently governing scholars' practices and experiences."[143] In view of globalization and internationalization, we need to revise our way of knowledge production and develop more diverse and just ways of research and publication. Lillis and Curry suggest a set of questions to make "visible ideologies of text production and evaluation systems."[144] These questions concern, for instance, the ideology of language (e.g., as a transparent medium), notions about rhetorical practices, what counts as global or local knowledge, and how decisions about relevance are made. While these questions could help reviewers and journals make culturally sensitive decisions, there is also the opportunity of language brokering, or journals offering support and mentoring for papers written by nonnative English speakers. Institutions such as universities or organizations (e.g., ISME) already offer support by native speakers for international scholars. To globalize music education, mutual mentoring might be a good way to connect scholars with different language competencies worldwide. It will be important to bring "the politics of English to the centre of debates around knowledge construction and to explore how 'conversations of the discipline' are refracted through the politics of language and location."[145] Globalizing music education in a culturally sensitive way will be successful only when as many voices as possible are included and also embrace the diversity of scholarly writing and research in music education.

The various conceptual elements presented in this chapter underline the significance of learning to think globally in music education research. This is one condition for globalizing music education and the further development of a global community. It helps us realize the challenges that we face as a professional community and scholarly discipline, also facilitating necessary transformations. We need to redefine who we are and who we want to be. Therefore, considering what it means to be global, and developing a global mindset, is a significant part of the formation of a united but diverse global music education community.

Notes

1. Jeremy Rappleye, *Educational Transfer in an Era of Globalization: Theory-History-Comparison* (New York: Peter Lang, 2012), 6.
2. Gita Steiner-Khamsi, "Understanding Policy Borrowing and Lending: Building Comparative Policy Studies," in *World Yearbook of Education 2012: Policy Borrowing and Lending in Education*, ed. Gita Steiner-Khamsi and Florian Waldow (New York: Routledge, 2012), 3–17.
3. David Phillips, "Policy Borrowing in Education: Frameworks for Analysis," in *International Handbook on Globalization, Education and Policy Research*, ed. Joseph Zajda (Dordrecht, Netherlands: Springer, 2005), 29.
4. Rappleye, *Educational Transfer*, 68–82.
5. Kimberly Ochs and David Phillips, "Processes of Educational Borrowing in Historical Context," in *Educational Policy Borrowing: Historical Perspectives*, ed. David Phillips and Kimberly Ochs (Oxford: Symposium Books, 2004), 16.
6. Rappleye, *Educational Transfer*, 66–82.
7. Ochs and Phillips, "Processes of Educational Borrowing in Historical Context," 10.
8. David Phillips, "Towards a Theory of Policy Attraction in Education," in *The Global Politics of Borrowing and Lending*, ed. Gita Steiner-Khamsi (New York: Teachers College Press, 2004), 59–61.
9. Roger Dale and Susan L. Robertson, "Towards a Critical Grammar of Education Policy Movement," in Steiner-Khamsi and Waldow, *World Yearbook of Education 2012*, 22.
10. Ibid., 28.
11. Steiner-Khamsi, "Understanding Policy Borrowing and Lending," 6–7.
12. Rappleye, *Educational Transfer*, 26–65.
13. The first publication explicitly addressing educational transfer in music education is Alexandra Kertz-Welzel, "Lessons from Elsewhere? Comparative Music Education in Times of Globalization," *Philosophy of Music Education Review* 23, no. 1 (2015): 48–66.
14. Bernarr Rainbow, "The Land with Music: Reality and Myth in Music Education," in *Bernarr Rainbow on Music*, ed. Peter Dickinson (Suffolk, UK: Boydell Press, 2012), 174–175.
15. Alexandra Kertz-Welzel, "The Singing Muse?" *Journal of Historical Research in Music Education* 26, no. 1 (2004): 18.
16. Harold J. Noah and Max A. Eckstein, *Toward a Science of Comparative Education* (London: Macmillan, 1969), 5.

17. Hullah's and Curwen's experiences also show that any borrowing has an impact on music education; even a failed attempt can transform music education. The report they published initiated a transformation of German music education, led by German musicologist Hermann Kretzschmar (1848–1924).

18. Masafumi Ogawa, "Japan: Music as a Tool for Moral Education?" in *The Origins and Foundations of Music Education*, ed. Gordon Cox and Robin Stevens (London: Continuum, 2010), 205.

19. Mekada Tanetaro (1853–1926), who was secretary general of the Ministry of Education, graduated from Harvard. Isawa Shuji (1851–1917), director of the Ministry of Education, studied at Bridgewater Normal School in Boston. See Ogawa, "Japan," 206.

20. Quoted in David Phillips, "Aspects of Educational Transfer," in *International Handbook of Comparative Education*, ed. Robert Cowen and Andreas M. Kazamias (Dordrecht, Netherlands: Springer, 2009), 1063.

21. There are two ways of educational borrowing that Phillips describes as "quick fix" and "phony": "Quick fix" means that new models are introduced because there is an immediate need for change and no room for time-consuming evaluations. This could happen after political revolutions but also after poor results in international student assessments. Using educational transfer for a quick fix of an educational system, to assure the public that politicians have tried to do something to change the situation, can be dangerous. "Phony" borrowing in the context of educational transfer is not so different from a quick fix: politicians announce changes loudly, using advertisement or political propaganda. It is not so much about whether education does de facto work or is useful but rather about the idea that politicians can solve problems. See David Phillips, "Policy Borrowing in Education: Frameworks for Analysis," in *International Handbook on Globalization, Education and Policy Research*, ed. Joseph Zajda (Dordrecht, Netherlands: Springer, 2005), 29.

22. Wilfried Gruhn, "European 'Methods' for American Nineteenth-Century Singing Instruction: A Cross-Cultural Perspective on Historical Research," *Journal of Historical Research in Music Education* 23, no. 1 (2001): 3–18.

23. Ibid., 15.

24. André de Quadros, ed., *Many Seeds, Different Flowers: The Musical Legacy of Carl Orff* (Nedlands: Callaway International Resource Centre for Music Education, University of Western Australia, 2000).

25. See Gordon Cox and Robin Stevens, *The Origins and Foundations of Music Education* (London: Continuum, 2010).

26. Roe-Min Kok, "Music for a Postcolonial Child: Theorizing Malaysian Memories," in *Learning, Teaching, and Musical Identity*, ed. Lucy Green (Bloomington: Indiana University Press, 2011), 73–90.

27. Alexander W. Wiseman and David P. Baker, "The Worldwide Explosion of Internationalized Education Policy," in *Global Trends in Educational Policy*, ed. David P. Baker and Alexander W. Wiseman (Amsterdam: Elsevier, 2005), 5.

28. El Sistema USA, "El Sistema in Venezuela," http://www.elsistemausa.org/el-sistema-in-venezuela.htm (accessed June 29, 2017).

29. Quoted in Tricia Tunstall, *Changing Lives: Gustavo Dudamel, El Sistema, and the Transformative Power of Music* (New York: W. W. Norton, 2012), 273.

30. Geoffrey Baker, "Editorial Introduction: El Sistema in Critical Perspective," *Action, Criticism and Theory for Music Education* 15, no. 1 (2016): 15, http://act.maydaygroup.org/articles/Baker15_1.pdf.

31. For more information, see Paul G. Woodford, *Re-thinking Standards for the Twenty-First Century: New Realities, New Challenges, New Propositions* (London: University of Western Ontario, 2011).

32. Gita Steiner-Khamsi, "Transferring Education, Displacing Reform," in *Discourse Formation in Comparative Education*, ed. Juergen Schriewer (Frankfurt, Germany: Peter Lang, 2000), 110–132.

33. Juergen Schriewer, "Globalization in Education: Process and Discourse," *Policy Futures in Education* 1, no. 2 (2003): 271–283.

34. Rappleye, *Educational Transfer*, 400–412.

35. Val D. Rust, "Foreign Influences in Educational Reform," in *Cross-National Attraction in Education: Accounts from England and Germany*, ed. Hubert Ertl (Oxford: Symposium Books, 2006), 26.

36. Rappleye, *Educational Transfer*, 400–432.

37. David H. Kamens, "Globalization and the Emergence of an Audit Culture: PISA and the Search for 'Best Practices' and Magic Bullets," in *PISA, Power and Policy: The Emergence of Educational Governance*, ed. Heinz-Dieter Mayer and Aaron Benavot (Oxford: Symposium Books, 2013), 130.

38. Ibid., 137.

39. The English translation of the title is "Plan and preliminary views for a work on comparative education."

40. Robert Cowen, "Comparing Futures or Comparing Pasts?" *Comparative Education* 36, no. 3 (2000): 335.

41. Rappleye, *Educational Transfer*, 112.

42. Stephen Carney, "Negotiating Policy in an Age of Globalization: Exploring Educational 'Policyscapes' in Denmark, Nepal, and China," *Comparative Education Review* 53, no. 1 (2009): 66.

43. David N. Wilson, "Comparative and International Education: Fraternal or Siamese Twins? A Preliminary Genealogy of Our Twin Fields," *Comparative Education Review* 4 (November 1994): 449.

44. Jeff Thompson, "International Education: Towards a Shared Understanding," *Journal of Research in International Education* 1, no. 1 (2002): 5.

45. Nelly P. Stromquist, "Comparative and International Education: A Journey Towards Equality and Equity," *Harvard Educational Review* 75, no. 1 (2005): 89.

46. Erwin H. Epstein, "Comparative and International Education: Overview and Historical Development," in *The International Encyclopedia of Education*, 2nd ed., ed. Torsten Husen (Oxford: Pergamon Press, 1994), 2:918.

47. "Many practitioners of international education are experts on international exchange and interaction. Their activities are partly based on a knowledge of comparative education." Ibid.

48. Robert Edward Hughes, *Schools at Home and Abroad* (London: Swan Sonnenschein, 1901), 2.

49. T. Neville Postlethwaite, "Preface," in *The Encyclopedia of Comparative Education and National Systems of Education*, ed. T. Neville Postlethwaite (Oxford: Pergamon Press, 1988), xvii.

50. George Z. F. Bereday, *Comparative Method in Education* (New York: Holt, Rinehart, and Winston 1964), 6.

51. Mark Bray, *Comparative Education: Continuing Traditions, New Challenges, and New Paradigms* (Dordrecht, Netherlands: Kluwer, 2003), 281.

52. Giovanni Sartori, "Compare Why and How: Comparing, Miscomparing and the Comparative Method," in *Comparing Nations: Concepts, Strategies, Substance*, ed. Mattei Dogan and Ali Kazancigil (Oxford: Blackwell, 1994), 17 (emphasis in original).

53. Mark Bray, Bob Adamson, and Mark Mason, *Comparative Education Research: Approaches and Methods* (Hong Kong: Springer, 2007).

54. Thomas Popkewitz, "Foreword," in Steiner-Khamsi, *The Global Politics of Educational Borrowing and Lending*, x.

55. Steiner-Khamsi, "Transferring Education, Displacing Reforms," 155–156.

56. Anthony E. Kemp and Laurence Lepherd, "Research Methods in International and Comparative Music Education," in *Handbook of Research on Music Teaching and Learning*, ed. Richard Colwell (New York: Schirmer Books, 1992), 777.

57. Harold J. Noah, "Comparative Education: Method," in *The Encyclopedia of Comparative Education and National Systems of Education*, ed. T. Neville Postlethwaite (Oxford: Pergamon Press 1988), 869.

58. Mark Bray and Murray R. Thomas, "Levels of Comparison in Educational Studies: Different Insights from Different Literatures and the Value of Multilevel Analysis," *Harvard Educational Review* 65, no. 3 (1995): 475.

59. Mark Bray, *Comparative Education: Continuing Traditions, New Challenges, and New Paradigms* (Dordrecht, Netherlands: Kluwer, 2003), 6.

60. Bereday, *Comparative Method in Education*, ix.

61. Ibid., 24.

62. Ibid.

63. Ibid., 28.

64. Alexandra Kertz-Welzel, "Music Education in the 21st Century: A Comparison of German and American Music Education Toward a New Concept of Global Exchange," *Music Education Research* 10, no. 4 (2008): 439–449.

65. Ibid., 441.

66. Bereday, *Comparative Method in Education*; Brian Holmes, *Problems in Education* (London: Routledge, 1965); Brian Holmes, *Comparative Education: Some Considerations of Method* (London: George Allen and Unwin, 1981).

67. Kemp and Lepherd, "Research Methods in International and Comparative Music Education," 777.

68. Brian Holmes, "Comparative Education," in *The Encyclopedia of Education*, ed. Lee C. Deighton (New York: Macmillan, 1971), 357.

69. Quoted in ibid., x.

70. Wilfried D. Halls, *Comparative Education: Contemporary Issues and Trends* (London: Jessica Kingsley, 1990), 22.

71. Quoted in David Phillips and Michele Schweisfurth, *Comparative and International Education: An Introduction to Theory, Method, and Practice* (London: Continuum, 2007), 11.

72. Ibid.

73. Quoted in ibid., 11–12.

74. Bereday, *Comparative Method in Education*, 143.

75. Patricia Potts, "The Place of Experience in Comparative Education Research," in Mark Bray, Bob Adamson, and Mark Mason, *Comparative Education Research: Approaches and Methods* (Hong Kong: Springer, 2007), 63–82.

76. Ibid., 81.

77. Phillips and Schweisfurth, *Comparative and International Education*, 53–56.

78. Yuefang Zhou et al., "Theoretical Models of Culture Shock and Adaptation in International Students in Higher Education," *Studies in Higher Education* 33, no. 1 (2008): 63–75.

79. Phillips and Schweisfurth, *Comparative and International Education*, 56.

80. Ibid., 53–56.

81. Chris Harrison and Sarah Hennessy, eds., *Listen Out: International Perspectives on Music Education* (Solihull, UK: National Association of Music Educators, 2012).

82. Johanne Schroeder, "Crossing Borders, Closing Gaps: In Favour of European Student Exchange in Music Education," in Harrison and Hennessy, *Listen Out*, 14–19.

83. Tomoko Ogusu, "Teaching Music in Different Cultural Contexts," in Harrison and Hennessy, *Listen Out*, 47–55.

84. James Garnett, "Young People's Experiences of Learning Music in Other Countries," in Harrison and Hennessy, *Listen Out*, 74–77.

85. Marie McCarthy, "International Perspectives," in *The Oxford Handbook of Music Education*, ed. Gary E. McPherson and Graham F. Welch (New York: Oxford University Press, 2012), 1:40.

86. Hildegard Froehlich, *A Social Theory for Music Education* (Lewiston, NY: Edwin Mellen, 2015), 226.

87. McCarthy, "International Perspectives," 42.

88. Cox and Stevens, *The Origins and Foundations of Music Education.*

89. Alexandra Kertz-Welzel, "Lesson Learned? In Search of Patriotism and Nationalism in the German Music Education Curriculum," in *Patriotism and Nationalism in Music Education*, ed. David G. Hebert and Alexandra Kertz-Welzel (Farnham, UK: Ashgate, 2012), 29.

90. Hebert and Kertz-Welzel, *Patriotism and Nationalism in Music Education.*

91. John Finney and Pamela Burnard, *Music Education with Digital Technology* (London: Continuum, 2007).

92. Bernd Clausen, *Der Hase im Mond: Studie zu japanischer Musik im japanischen Musikunterricht* [The hare in the moon: A survey on Japanese music in Japanese music education] (Berlin: LIT, 2009).

93. McCarthy, "International Perspectives," 55.

94. Jonathan Parquette, "Theories of Professional Identity: Bringing Cultural Policy in Perspective," in *Cultural Policy, Work and Identity: The Creation, Renewal and Negotiation of Professional Subjectivities*, ed. Jonathan Parquette (Farnham, UK: Ashgate, 2012), 4.

95. Wayne Bowman, "Who Is the 'We'? Rethinking Professionalism in Music Education," *Action, Criticism and Theory for Music Education* 6, no. 4 (2007): 110–114, http://act.maydaygroup.org/articles/Bowman6_4.pdf.

96. Ibid., 116.

97. Ibid., 119.

98. Ibid.

99. Ibid., 120.

100. Ibid., 115.

101. Hildegard Froehlich, "Music Education and Community: Reflections on 'Webs of Interaction' in School Music," *Action, Criticism and Theory for Music Education* 8, no. 1 (2009): 92, http://act.maydaygroup.org/articles/Froehlich8_1.pdf.

102. Ibid., 94.

103. Ibid.

104. Benedict Anderson, *Imagined Communities* (London: Verso, 2006), 6.

105. Ken Hyland, *Disciplinary Identities: Individuality and Community in Academic Discourse* (Cambridge: Cambridge University Press, 2012), 22.

106. Tony Becher, *Academic Tribes and Territories: Intellectual Enquiry and the Cultures of Disciplines* (Bristol, UK: Open University Press, 1989), 24.

107. Ibid.

108. Burton R. Clark, "Academic Culture" (working paper no. 42, Yale University Higher Education Research Group, 1980), 1.

109. Alexandra Kertz-Welzel, "Internationalisierung und musikpaedagogische Wissenschaftskulturen: Eine Annaeherung" [Internationalization and academic culture in music education: An approach], *Zeitschrift fuer Kritische Musikpaedagogik* [Journal of critical music education] 3 (2015): 35–48, http://zfkm.org/sonder15-kertz-welzel.pdf.

110. Estelle R. Jorgensen, *Transforming Music Education* (Bloomington: Indiana University Press, 2003).

111. David J. Elliott, *Music Matters: A New Philosophy of Music Education* (New York: Oxford University Press, 1995).

112. Patricia Shehan Campbell, *Songs in Their Heads: Music and Its Meaning in Children's Lives*, 2nd ed. (New York: Oxford University Press, 2010).

113. Gary E. McPherson and Graham F. Welch, *Oxford Handbook of Music Education* (Oxford: Oxford University Press, 2012).

114. For more information, see the journal's website, at https://scholarworks.iu.edu/iupjournals/index.php/pmer.

115. For more information, see the organization's website, at http://ispme.net.

116. Theresa Lillis and Mary Jane Curry, *Academic Writing in a Global Context: The Politics and Practices of Publishing in English* (New York: Routledge, 2010), 6.

117. Ken Hyland, *Academic Publishing: Issues and Challenges in the Construction of Knowledge* (Oxford: Oxford University Press, 2015), 35.

118. Stuart Hall, "The Local and the Global: Globalization and Ethnicity," in *Culture, Globalization and the World System*, ed. Anthony D. King (Minneapolis: University of Minnesota Press, 1997), 19–40.

119. Enlightenment and its impact on our understanding of knowledge, science, and society have been criticized by philosophers such as Max Horckheimer, Theodor Adorno, and Michel Foucault. See Max Horckheimer and Theodor W. Adorno, *Dialectic of Enlightenment*, trans. by Edmund Jephcott (Stanford, CA: Stanford University Press, 2002); and Michel Foucault, *The Order of Things* (London: Tavistock, 1970).

120. Hyland, *Academic Publishing*, 35.

121. Athelstan Suresh Canagarajah, "Reconstructing Local Knowledge, Reconfiguring Language Studies," in *Reclaiming the Local in Language, Policy and Practice*, ed. Athelstan Suresh Canagarajah (Mahwah, NJ: Lawrence Erlbaum, 2005), 5.

122. Sandra Bermann, *A Companion to Translation Studies* (Chichester, UK: Wiley-Blackwell, 2014).

123. Alexandra Kertz-Welzel, "Didaktik of Music: A German Concept and Its Comparison to American Music Pedagogy," *International Journal of Music Education (Practice)* 22, no. 3 (2004): 277–286.

124. Penny Enslin and Kai Horsthemke, "Can *Ubuntu* Provide a Model for Citizenship Education in African Democracies?," *Comparative Education* 40, no. 4 (2004): 545–558.

125. See Elliott, *Music Matters*.

126. Hanne Fossum and Oivind Varkoy, "The Changing Concept of Aesthetic Experience in Music Education," *Nordic Research in Music Education Yearbook* 14 (2012): 9–25.

127. Alexandra Kertz-Welzel, "Musikpaedagogische Grundbegriffe und die Internationalisierung der Musikpaedagogik: Ein unloesbares Dilemma?" [Basic ideas in music education and internationalization: An insoluble dilemma?], in *(Grund-)Begriffe musikpaedagogischen Nachdenkens: Entstehung, Bedeutung, Gebrauch* [Basic ideas in music education: Development, meaning, use], ed. Juergen Vogt, Frauke Hess, and Markus Brenk (Münster, Germany: LIT, 2014), 19–35.

128. Anna Mauranen, "Cultural Differences in Academic Discourse: Problems of a Linguistic and Cultural Minority," in *The Competent Intercultural Communicator*, ed. L. Löfman, L.

Kurki-Suonio, S. Pellinen, and J. Lehtonen (Jyväskylä: Finnish Association of Applied Linguistics, 1993), 157–174, http://www.afinla.fi/sites/afinla.fi/files/1993Mauranen.pdf.

129. Robert Kaplan, "Cultural Thought Patterns in Intercultural Education," *Language Learning* 16, no. 1 (1966): 2.

130. Ibid., 4.

131. Alexandra Kertz-Welzel, "'Two Souls, Alas, Reside within My Breast': Reflections on German and American Music Education regarding the Internationalization of Music Education," *Philosophy of Music Education Review* 21, no. 1 (2013): 52–65.

132. For more information about universities, see Clark Kerr, *The Uses of the University*, 5th ed. (Cambridge, MA: Harvard University Press, 2001).

133. Winfried Thielmann, *Deutsche und englische Wissenschaftssprache im Vergleich: Hinfuehren, Verknuepfen, Benennen* [A comparison of German and English academic language: Introducing, relating, designating] (Heidelberg, Germany: Synchron, 2009).

134. Ibid., 72.

135. Ibid., 89–227.

136. Hyland, *Academic Publishing*, 172.

137. Anna Mauranen, Carmen Perez-Llantada, and John M. Swales, "Academic Englishes: A Standardized Knowledge?," in *The Routledge Handbook of World Englishes*, ed. Andy Kirkpatrick (New York: Routledge, 2010), 638.

138. Lillis and Curry, *Academic Writing in a Global Context*, 155.

139. Mauranen, Perez-Llantada, and Swales, "Academic Englishes," 639.

140. Lillis and Curry, *Academic Writing in a Global Context*, 152.

141. Ibid., 159.

142. Ibid., 143 (emphasis in original).

143. Ibid., 155.

144. Ibid., 162.

145. Ibid., 23–24.

3 Developing a Global Mindset

GLOBALIZATION AND INTERNATIONALIZATION affect music education world-wide. They challenge our common notions of music teaching and learning and require transformations on the institutional, the pedagogical, and the individual levels. Most of all, we have to learn how to come to terms with diversity. We need to address it in research and teaching, helping our students learn to deal with the multiplicity of music education and research cultures around the globe. While this is certainly no easy task, music education is not the first discipline to face these challenges. Research from various fields such as intercultural education can help in developing concepts for music education with regard to transcultural competence or a global mindset. It is important to develop these competencies to globalize music education in a way not only embracing diversity but also using its benefits.

This chapter investigates what it means to be global, with regard to three conceptual elements: international music education policy, the music classroom, and the global mindset. They illustrate ways of shaping the formation of a united and diverse global music education community in terms of globalizing music education.

International Music Education Policy

There seems to be one global commonality among music educators with which everybody who has spent some time working in schools is familiar: many music teachers like to complain about administration, curricula, teaching duties, salary, the constant need for justification, or a lack of acknowledgment. This global discontent of music educators raises questions: Who is responsible for the bad state of affairs? Why do music educators worldwide think they are helpless and blame somebody else for their daily problems? What should be changed so that music educators feel empowered and would have opportunities to transform the system they are working in? These and many more issues are part of the field of music education policy. It is concerned with administrative and political aspects of music education but also aims at empowering music teachers to be part of decision-making processes in order to transform their labor conditions. Reconsidering music education policy in view of globalization is therefore crucial and can facilitate globalizing music education.

What Is Music Education Policy?

It is not easy to describe what music education policy is. One of the reasons is a lack of research, because it was not part of a specific field of research but rather "falls in the crack between arts policy and educational policy."[1] However, in general, music education policy is focused on the provision of education, particularly regarding the constitutional and administrative framework. It is concerned with standards for teacher education, curriculum design, assessment, budget issues, or music education advocacy. It connects music education with the state and the public. Policy and policies are thereby twofold: they deal with values a society has but also with actions resulting from these values and the framework they imply. Anne Schneider and Helen Ingram emphasize:

> Policies are the mechanisms through which values are authoritatively allocated for society. Policies are revealed through texts, practices, symbols and discourses that define and deliver values including goods and services, regulation, income and status.[2]

Policy and policies represent the beliefs a society has and that it preserves in documents, laws, and curricula. They provide "guidelines for actions that match the complex understandings, views, and positions with the discrete realities of an issue."[3] Music education curricula are a good example for the nature of these documents: They present the cultural values a society has and suggest ways students should become acquainted with them in music education. Curricula structure processes of musical learning and try to ensure that, statewide or nationwide, similar standards are applied. They are important music education policy documents and indicate that music education policy is connected to the classroom.

While it is not easy to determine what music education policy is, Patrick Schmidt might be right in asserting that the only way to really know what it is, is by doing it.[4] However, musicians, music educators, and scholars have long been reluctant to participate in music education policy: First, many musicians and music educators prefer to be focused on music and teaching, leaving the real world to politicians and administrators. Second, those musicians who are interested in issues such as policy and social justice often do not have the basic knowledge, skills, or connections necessary for successfully engaging in music education policy. Third, because they do not know how decision-making and implementation processes in music education policy work, many of those music educators who do engage in music education policy are disappointed because they sometimes do not reach their goals. Often, either the original agenda has been changed by stakeholders, lobbyists, or political circumstances or the implementation process has not worked out in the expected way. But even if musicians and scholars might not be naturally attracted to music education policy, Patrick Jones is right when he states that public policy and music education policy are "too important to trust strictly to legislators and government officials who can change priorities based on party politics, leaders of the music products and professional arts industries whose main interests are sales of their products, or to simply leave to chance."[5] Leaving music education policy to people not acquainted with music education can be dangerous, because they are often driven by motivations that are not always focused on what is best for music education. More music educators and scholars need to be active in music education policy, no matter how frustrating it might be at first. To facilitate their political engagement and to ensure that politicians act in music education's best interest, Jones makes some suggestions. First, there is a need for research to provide the foundation for a public music education policy. This would ensure that it is research-based, guaranteeing "that the intended and enacted policies result in universal access to music education."[6] Creating this research is certainly no easy task for the music education policy community. The danger of oversimplification and generalization, exemplified in arguments such as the Mozart effect, is well known. To convince the public, politicians often need easily accessible proposals that everybody understands. Connecting research in music education policy and public politics is also a matter of learning to speak the language of politicians while observing scholarly standards. This concerns the training of a "cadre of policy experts" who are able to communicate with both sides:[7] On the one hand, they have to conduct research in music education policy as well as convincing fellow music educators and scholars of the value of engaging in music education policy. On the other hand, they have to speak the language of politicians without compromising music education's best interest.

When discussing music education policy, it is also important to take into account internationalization. Because of developments in education, international student assessments, and the significance international organizations such as the Organization for Economic Cooperation and Development (OECD) or the World Bank have for the funding of educational projects, it is important to consider music education policy as an international endeavor. We are a global community and face similar challenges and opportunities. Marie McCarthy identifies some of the aspects that music education worldwide faces in terms of the status of music education, music education advocacy, curriculum development, whose music is school music, the culture of pedagogy, and professional networks.[8] She argues that the global community is much better prepared than a single national tradition of music education to address these challenges and to turn them into opportunities. Most of the issues McCarthy identifies as international challenges are part of the field of music education policy. They concern the administrative and constitutional foundations of music education. This points out how important music education policy is internationally. McCarthy states, while referring to the "global tapestry of music education," that music education is "a shared social responsibility."[9] Realizing that we can be successful only as a global community will be important for the future of the music education profession:

> The profession's response to this reality will determine the sustainability and direction of music education in the future decades. Groups such as UNESCO and ISME play an increasingly important role in developing awareness of this responsibility, but it also resides in the actions of individual teachers and national organizations.[10]

While certainly every music educator has an impact on the future of music education by his or her actions, McCarthy also points out the significance of national and international organizations. While UNESCO is focused on education, culture, and research in general, ISME is concerned only with music, including building and maintaining a global music education community. Established in 1953 and originally motivated by the hope that "music as an international language of humankind could serve to unite people of differing viewpoints and perspectives,"[11] ISME indeed supports the formation of a worldwide music education community. International conferences and preconference meetings of ISME commissions, including the ISME Commission on Music Policy: Culture, Education and Media,[12] try to foster the development of a global music education community.

But apart from international organizations, national organizations also play a major role in music education policy, whether the German Music Council (Deutscher Musikrat) with its state-based organizations[13] or the American National Association for Music Education (NAfME), representing American music education and music educators.[14] While these organizations are intensely engaged in music education advocacy, there are also critical issues related to them. Many stakeholders and lobbyists are involved in such organizations and follow their own agendas, sometimes not focused on music education's best interests. Additionally, the music industry is a powerful player in organizations and music education advocacy, trying to sell products—no matter whether instruments or textbooks—and attempting to have an impact on the direction of large regional or national music education organizations. This indicates that music education policy and advocacy can be double-edged and that music teachers and scholars need to be aware of this ambivalence.

Advocacy and Political Decision-Making Processes

Music education advocacy tries to convince the public, administrators, boards of education, or politicians of the benefits of music education. The job of advocates, as Michael Mark and Patrice Madura put it, is "to inform decision makers about the importance of arts education, how proposed legislation will affect arts education and what legislation is needed to improve or correct problems related to the field.”[15] One of the tools used is research demonstrating the value of music education in schools. This is not unproblematic, because it can mean referring to controversial studies supporting nonmusical goals of music education, such as studies on the Mozart effect or, in Germany, the Bastian study, which indicates that additional music lessons help improve social behavior and creativity.[16] Utilitarian and nonmusical goals are most convincing for politicians and the public, as the music-makes-you-smarter movement, popularizing the Mozart effect, proves.[17] Politicians sometimes need easily accessible facts or stories of success, such as those of the El Sistema project, to convince the public that money spent for music education is well invested. Purely musical goals, such as enjoying music and its aesthetic value, understanding and creating music, or experiencing flow while performing or listening, might not be immediately convincing in a political environment in which there is intense competition for funding. In fact, music education policy is certainly not the most prominent area in public policy. It is sometimes overlooked, because music educators and scholars are rarely able to speak the language of politicians. But for successful advocacy work, it is necessary to be affiliated with the political sphere and to be familiar with some of its rules. Hildegard Froehlich correctly emphasizes that the starting point for successful music education advocacy is turning a private interest into a public one.[18] Music education is important not only to some people or a special interest group but for everybody. Politicians and the public will listen to topics that concern everyone.

Turning a private into a public interest particularly means understanding how decision-making processes in policy work. Froehlich, therefore, distinguishes two models of decision making in policy as identified by political analysts, the stepwise model and the "swirling" model.[19] The stepwise model follows a rather linear path. The first stage is the setting of an agenda, when gaining the public's interest is necessary. A popular leader should be identified who supports the agenda and presents it, both to the public and to his or her fellow leaders and politicians. This first stage is a crucial one, because many private interest groups are not able to find a politician to represent them and gain the interest of the public. In the second stage, policy formation and legitimization, representatives of the government, a parliament, or special networks, organizations, or interest groups are involved. They work on a specific policy, advised by music educators, scholars, or educationalists. The composition of the group is important because the individual background of the members has an impact on the policy. This group usually develops a draft. This draft will be discussed and eventually voted on by officials. Froehlich describes this process:

> A public policy is legitimized once it is formally passed by the decision-making body. That is, ideas do not become policies until some formal action is taken by

elected officials. The formal action of legitimization may be a law enacted by a legislative body or a rule laid down by a bureaucratic agency.[20]

For many musicians, music educators, or scholars, this decision-making process in music education policy is not clear. It is a crucial task for music teacher education programs to equip their students with the necessary knowledge and skills to participate successfully in music education policy. This would also facilitate the third stage, the implementation of a policy, after it is voted on and passed by the legislative—for instance, a parliament. Putting a policy into practice depends on various factors. It is particularly important to find out who is in charge of providing the necessary funding for the implementation of a policy. Sometimes, even though a decision-making body might pass a policy, it is not responsible for providing the funding for implementation. In other cases, politicians or administrators might need help or advice in carrying out the respective policy because they are not familiar with the arts or music. Froehlich encourages music educators and scholars to be part of this process:

> Since implementation often falls upon state educational bureaucracies, music educators need to be aware that government workers unfamiliar with the arts may not have the professional knowledge needed to make the best choices in the implementation phase. Action informed by the knowledge and experience of professionals in the area is therefore essential.[21]

Music educators and scholars should not leave the implementation of a policy to other groups but rather be part of the entire process of implementation. Their expertise is vital if the implementation of a policy is to be successful.

While the stepwise model implies that decision-making processes in policy follow a rather linear outline, there also is another point of view, the swirling model. It emphasizes that this seemingly logical and sequential process is not always what happens in music education policy. Froehlich explains:

> The policy making process should rather be linked to a cauldron or a whirlpool in which problems and solutions swirl around over time and solutions may arise before the problem actually makes it onto the public agenda. It also suggests that time, space, and place of decision-making have important functions in such a cauldron.[22]

This model uncovers the often complicated and chaotic way political decisions are made. Special events sometimes change the order of steps; new problems occur or are solved. Sudden opportunities that arise out of new circumstances can also destroy a stepwise organization of political decision making. Froehlich emphasizes that it is important with regard to the swirling model that all stakeholders and participants are permanently open and alert for new opportunities: "Only constant watchfulness can bring about timely feedback and opportune political action."[23] Music teachers and scholars who participate in this process need to have the basic knowledge about political decision-making processes, also accepting frustrating phases in view of the perspective that everything might work out, eventually.

These two models of decision making indicate what the challenges for music teachers and scholars are in music education policy. They need to be familiar with the processes and steps of political decision making, constantly evaluating the situation and recognizing emerging opportunities. Above all, it is crucial to be affiliated with politicians, members of parliament, or leaders of interest groups to maintain "communicative channels."[24] In fact, these personal relationships might be the most important factor in successful music education policy work. However, when it comes to implementing a policy, different means are needed.

The Problem of Implementation

Although a political decision-making process might result in a desirable policy, this does not mean that it changes anything in music education classrooms. A policy needs to be implemented, to be put into practice. This is a complex endeavor and concerns many levels and people. Michael Fullan and Suzanne Stiegelbauer are right when they state that "educational change is technically simple, but socially complex."[25] For successful implementation, several factors need to be taken into account. Chi Cheung Leung summarizes:

> Policy implementation involves unavoidable constraints, complex networking and coordination, negotiation and communication, attitude changes of various stakeholders, mobilization of resources and provision of support, and timely schedule planning and sequencing.[26]

While many factors have an impact on the effectiveness of policy implementation, people involved in the process of implementation play a major role. The readiness of stakeholders, administrators, and teachers is essential. But available facilities, time, or financial resources are significant, too. Using networks also supports the implementation, as do the management skills of people involved in the process. However, since people are the crucial factor, one of the most important tasks in successful implementation is to convince the public, administrators, and teachers of the need for a new policy. Music educators who are reluctant to have a new policy can stop every implementation.

On the basis of two case studies, in Australia and Hong Kong, Leung develops a theoretical framework for effective policy implementation.[27] He identifies six important factors: leadership, school culture and value, management, communication, environment and resources, and time and timing. Regarding leadership, it is crucial that somebody has a vision and goals and takes "initiative and empowerment based on informed theory, knowledge, and expertise with supportive strategy, persuasion and decision making."[28] But the core ideas of a leader should match the school culture and its values and should particularly refer to specific needs that a school has and that a new policy would meet. An accuracy of fit is important. Good management facilitates the implementation of a policy through effective coordination and organization. Communication and negotiations are also crucial, supporting continuous evaluation and adjustment. Providing sufficient resources and creating a positive environment in which everybody is engaged and is acknowledged for his or her achievements in the process of policy implementation is important as well. Finally, time and timing are significant factors. The implementation of a policy might take longer than expected.

While Leung's model, emphasizing the significance of collaboration and discourse, is certainly convincing, each process of implementation has its own challenges. Liane Hentschke supports this observation by referring to the implementation of a music education policy in Brazil:[29] Even though music education became a compulsory subject from kindergarten to secondary school in 2008, it was not possible to turn this policy into practice, although the political intention was to have it implemented by 2011. Some of the factors Leung identified were indeed problematic. While turning music education into a mandatory subject in public schools was a desirable policy, Brazilian universities were not prepared to train as many new teachers as necessary to meet the needs created by the new policy. Transformations in music teacher education and programs would have been necessary and also more funding. This was not possible to accomplish in three years. Additionally, many schools were reluctant to implement the new policy, arguing, for instance, that they already had arts education in their curriculum and that there was no need for transformations. A problem in Brazil is also that "few mechanisms exist to ensure that what is being taught is in accordance with federal policies."[30] If no organization or administration oversees the implementation process, most schools will stay with what they have always done, referring to its success and popularity. Politicians are often not interested in the process of implementation, particularly if they have superficial notions about music and musicality. Hentschke states, "From a social standpoint, in the eyes of many policy makers, Brazilians are a very musical people, and consequently, there is little need to bring music into the schools."[31] Stereotypical notions like these can jeopardize the successful implementation of a policy. Research in music education policy needs to address these issues and to facilitate a more reflective approach.

The problems discussed by Hentschke regarding the implementation of a music education policy are certainly not unique to Brazil. Rather, there are similar problems worldwide. Hentschke thus argues for an increased engagement in international music education policy and advocacy. For her, this concerns particularly the exchange of information about music education, policy, and advocacy. She states:

> There is a sense of urgency regarding the potentially negative impact of the current lack of cross-national knowledge on the state of arts education and the capacity of that lack of knowledge to influence both practice and policy.[32]

Not having sufficient knowledge about music education policy in some countries diminishes the power the global music education community has. We need to emphasize the commonalities so that politicians or administrators cannot marginalize music education in any country. Hentschke considers publications by UNESCO and other international organizations as important points of reference for this endeavor, such as the "Road Map for Arts Education."[33] This report, which was presented at the first UNESCO World Conference for Arts Education in Lisbon in 2006, tries to provide a foundation for arts education and advocacy, emphasizing arts' significance for people's lives and describing its aims, important concepts and essential strategies, research, and case studies. The road map aims at informing politicians and administrators but also music educators, scholars, and everybody interested in arts education and advocacy. Its main intentions are to help stakeholders in particular orient themselves in developing national or local policies. To encourage music educators worldwide to use the tools of advocacy for strengthening our power as a global community is important for the future of music education. Anne Bamford states:

> There is an abundance of research on the positive impacts of the arts in education, and a history of humanity including the arts as it teaches the young, but all this is of limited impact if it is not backed by strategic action to enable full implementation. We must have the confidence, capacity, optimism and faith to change things beyond individual schools. By communicating with others we will create a culture where teachers and leaders will take responsibility for making improvements in their own schools and in others.[34]

Music teachers and scholars need to be engaged in music education policy, using the research available indicating the transformative power of music. In the field of policy, success often depends on being well connected. When everybody is part of the implementation process and feels empowered, knowing that individual opinions and actions matter and that we are all part of a global community, then there will be no need to feel discouraged and to blame others for problems. Music education policy is an international field of research and practice that empowers and recruits people to be part of the decision-making and implementation processes. Realizing and circulating this claim will significantly transform music education worldwide and help address successfully the challenges globalization poses. Therefore, international music education policy is a significant part of a conceptual framework facilitating globalizing music education. This also concerns the development of a global music classroom, a space where encountering musical diversity and practicing lifelong musical engagement is important.

The Global Music Classroom

Globalization has changed music education in many ways. A significant transformation, due to constant mobility or frequent changes of workplaces, concerns the space where musical learning happens. In common images of music education, schools, private studios, and teachers were almost indispensable. Today, a more flexible meaning of musical learning is usual because it can happen everywhere. Knowledge about the benefits of informal learning and the constant advancement of technology, facilitating self-initiated musical activities, have supported this development.[35] This also leads to new definitions of what musical creativity is in relation to various kinds of musical engagement.[36] When considering what musical learning, in view of globalization, looks like, it is important to realize that the global music classroom is above all a virtual entity, being able to materialize wherever musical learning happens. It can concern musical engagement inside and outside schools and in all varieties of settings, places, and circumstances. The global music classroom is shaped by the diversity of musical cultures, individual or communal musical worlds, and lifelong learning. As a space for musically encountering oneself and others, it is essential for surviving in times of globalization and the often-unpredictable impact this has on our lives. It is a place to retreat to and musically master the challenges globalization poses.

Global Childhoods

Globalization shapes children's lives in different ways: On the one hand, children in Germany have experiences similar to those in Australia regarding, for example, popular music, fashion, food, and media. On the other hand, they live in different worlds, still dominated by national, regional, or local traditions. This ambiguity of children's experiences needs to be taken into account when considering the musical worlds in which children live and the contributions music education inside and outside schools can make.

In children's studies, the term *global childhood* stands for "the idea that children in different parts of the world share similar experiences of childhood."[37] This might concern general characteristics of childhood, such as physical immaturity, dependency on adults, or the special features of childhood as mentioned in the UN Convention on the Rights of the Child.[38] It is also related to the "corporate construction of childhood" as intended by major companies, using the media to create the global child as consumer.[39] But research indicates that, despite global commonalities, childhoods are diverse, depending on the country and the culture children grow up in. Some researchers even state that the general notion of childhood is Western-derived and implies a kind of phase in life that is common only to children in wealthy countries.[40] Children in other parts of the world, many of them being required to work to secure the survival of their families, have different childhoods. There certainly is no standardized child or childhood. Karen Wells might be correct when stating that "the global becomes one of several structures . . . that shape the lives of children and concepts of childhood in any specific socio-cultural setting."[41]

However, the important role music plays in children's lives is certainly a global commonality. Children use music of the global popular music culture and music of their national, regional, or local traditions to create their own musical identities. By merging different musical cultures, they often create transcultural musical identities.[42] Patricia Shehan Campbell and Trevor Wiggins underline that "children may act globally by virtue of their development passage, but think locally."[43] Both global and local aspects are important to support the development of children's musical identities, often balancing different musical influences as part of their own diverse cultural heritage. Whether through the Yakama Nation Tribal School in Washington State, which helps young people connect with their Native American heritage,[44] bicultural education in New Zealand[45] or Hong Kong,[46] children and young people learn to merge various musical cultures and influences into their own musical identities. Children's musical cultures and identities are indeed influenced by global and national, regional, or local elements. Campbell and Wiggins summarize that "the emphasis given to diversity over commonality has prevented the examination of patterns of children's practices, when in fact childhood may best be viewed for its global as well as cultural-specific entities."[47] Kathryn Marsh's research on children's musical games in playgrounds and schoolyards worldwide supports these findings.[48]

This hybrid mixture of musical cultures in children's musical worlds demonstrates one notion that is significant in view of globalization: transculturality. The German philosopher Wolfgang Welsch (b. 1946) originally developed this concept to underline that globalization leads to a cultural mix and that traditional notions of cultures as distinct entities do not match our situation today.[49] He argues that we are cultural hybrids and need to find our individual ways of integrating cultural influences into our personal identity. This concept is easily applicable to children's musical cultures:

> Often, children's abilities to merge various cultures, particularly the global and the local, are far more evolved than the respective skills that adults have. This ability to create hybrid or transcultural identities could be an example for a much-needed skill to overcome the problems of globalization.[50]

Children's musical cultures and identities are places where they mix cultural influences and reconcile them. They know how to use music for their own purposes, learn from others, and share music and can design a transcultural musical identity that matches their feelings and beliefs. This process can be supported by music education in schools or be the result of informal musical activities.

Addressing Musical Diversity

Young people in today's globalized world constantly encounter different cultures and have to make sense of these experiences. Multicultural music education has been a well-known way to exemplarily learn how to deal with different cultures in the domain of music. Instructional goals range from simply getting to know musical cultures to fostering intercultural understanding or tolerance. Depending on the history of a country and its music education, different approaches have been developed. In Germany, music education concerned with music of various cultures has usually been called *interkulturelle Musikpaedagogik* (intercultural music education). This indicates that the vision of German society was not as a multicultural but rather an intercultural and dialogic one, certainly welcoming other cultures, while being focused on a German core culture (*Leitkultur*) as point of reference.[51] The first approach to intercultural music education in Germany was the *Schnittstellenansatz* (interface approach) of the 1980s, developed by German music education scholar Irmgard Merkt (b. 1946).[52] At the core of this concept is the significance of meeting points among musical cultures as a way of initiating dialogue. Joint music making is the starting point for experiencing what unites and distinguishes us, later leading to discussions about significant dimensions of music and life in various cultures. Merkt's interface approach underlines that concepts addressing diversity in music education are rooted in the sociocultural context of a specific country. There is not just one approach of multicultural music education worldwide but many. Most often, we tend to overlook this fact. In view of globalization and internationalization, it is crucial to point out that our perspectives on music of various cultures in music education depend on the sociocultural context or the respective educational system. There certainly is no one solution that fits all for multicultural music education around the globe.[53] But this does not mean that we cannot learn from each other. However, we have to be sensitive to cultural contexts and adapt approaches in appropriate ways. One of the benefits of globalization and internationalization is the chance to get to know approaches from many cultures. This offers opportunities for finding the most appropriate and culturally sensitive concepts that support young people's musical development in view of cultural complexity.

Campbell's approach as presented in her book *Teaching Music Globally* is certainly one of these culturally sensitive approaches that can be used in music education internationally.[54] By passing through stages such as sound awareness, attentive listening, engaged listening, and enactive listening and, finally, creating world music, students become able to actively shape the way they encounter the music of various cultures. Listening in the way Campbell intends is not passive but rather active musical engagement, "utilizing listening as the guide to stylistically appropriate performance."[55] At each stage, students become more involved—for example, in engaged listening, such as drumming rhythmic patterns or singing along, enactive listening in terms of performing a piece that was aurally learned, and creating world music as a way of improvising in the style of the music encountered. This approach gives students many opportunities to use their own musical experiences and ways of learning. By placing listening in terms of aural and oral learning at the center of this multicultural music education approach, Campbell uses traditional ways of learning, as used in many cultures around the world and in informal learning practices in popular music. Campbell states that it can be "challenging for students to learn music that is new to their ears, and listening alone can be a time-consuming pathway to learning music for performance."[56] But in the end, it is worth renouncing notation, particularly because it is often not able to capture all the dimensions of sound. This way of learning music is also close to young people's informal music practices in popular music, even though it certainly raises well-known issues of authenticity in world music classrooms. Learning music through listening and imitation helps students gain the competencies needed for self-directed musical activities supporting the appreciation of music of various cultures. These are much-needed competencies in times of globalization. Campbell's approach clearly tries to respect the variety of musical cultures worldwide and the way they are taught. It does not treat them like artworks of the classical music tradition, being focused on notation as the precondition for performing. Rather, it understands music as a vivid document of distinct cultures. Creating music in the style of a musical tradition encountered fosters the development of students' musical creativity and helps them be self-determined learners. Knowing how to approach cultural diversity in music might also help young people master the diversity they encounter in other parts of their lives.

Culturally sensitive approaches acknowledging diversity are crucial for music education in view of globalization and for globalizing music education. This also means taking into account such aspects as antiracist education, trying to overcome unconsciously perpetuated concepts of race in multicultural music education.[57] This includes questioning hidden Eurocentric hierarchies in defining what world music is, particularly in relation to classical music, and the quest for ethical and culturally sensitive encounters with music of various cultures.[58] These and many more approaches underline that it is certainly no easy task to address musical diversity in music education in a global world. Much more research is needed to overcome our sometimes oversimplified assumptions. Merkt's and Campbell's approaches, as well as the concepts of many researchers worldwide, are just starting points, exemplifying the need for more reflective and culturally sensitive approaches. It is particularly important to enable students to be self-determined learners, using self-initiated musical activities for encountering the music of various cultures in their lifelong musical learning endeavor.

Lifelong Musical Engagement

Because of globalization, the individual lives of people are often influenced by frequent changes of workplaces and the need for constantly acquiring new knowledge and skills. The pressure to function perfectly in whatever occupation or country a person finds herself creates a need for having a place where one can be oneself and recharge. Therefore, music plays an important role in the lives of many adults as a place to which they can retreat.[59] No matter what kind of musical engagement people prefer, whether listening, singing in a choir, playing in a band, learning guitar through video tutorials, or presenting compositions in an online forum, musical activities and learning are meaningful. Musical engagement today is versatile, often related to informal learning or self-initiated music making, involving creativity, and happening in communities or alone. Pamela Burnard points out that, today, acknowledging diverse musical creativities is essential, whether jointly composing in a band, DJing, or developing an individual arrangement of a song with software such as GarageBand. Particularly technology helps mediate musical creativities, offering "young people modes of musical participation, increased access to music, and tools for mediating their musical experiences."[60] The internet represents a space for exploration or communication, offers information, and gives opportunities for composing, improvising, or playing in virtual music-making contexts. Digital musicianship is a significant part of people's musical worlds today, also situating the global music classroom as a virtual space, mediated by technology and connecting people worldwide. Music education certainly has to prepare young people for digital musicianship, including helping them be self-determined and critical regarding digital media, using the knowledge they already have and supplementing it.[61] This facilitates lifelong musical engagement.

Even though musical engagement and learning in terms of the global music classroom happen everywhere, music education in schools is still special. For some children, it is the first opportunity for musical activities and systematic musical learning, shaping belief systems, attitudes, preferences, and expectations. It offers chances to acquire musical knowledge and skills but also to encounter new kinds of music. Music education in schools has to address several tasks. On the one hand, it is about immediate engagement and enjoyment of music. On the other hand, it is also about acquiring musical skills and knowledge facilitating lifelong musical activities. However, preparing young people for lifelong musical engagement is not an unproblematic objective for music education in public schools, because of the preference for short-term goals in terms of the next exam or recital. Stephanie Pitts asserts:

Few head teachers, school governors, or indeed parents would be persuaded that the benefits of learning in school will reach fruition many years later: the emphasis as young people leave schools is on assessing what they can do now, not on the more challenging questions of how their formative years might shape them as adults.[62]

Preparing students for lifelong musical engagement might involve a shift in music education policy, as well as public expectations. This can mean learning to appreciate that music educators might in some areas teach only very basic skills (e.g., playing guitar, ear training, using music software) and also helping students become familiar with online resources or community music activities. While the competencies and skills students are able to acquire might be only in the beginning stages, they promise further development and facilitate lifelong musical engagement. Though this should certainly not be the only goal of music education in schools, it is an important one, particularly when supported by student-centered activities in classrooms. David Myers states, regarding music education's goal of lifelong musical engagement, that "the focus must be on engaging children in independent and authentic music-making that is consistent with their developmental capacities, and that will grow with them into and through adulthood."[63] Teacher-directed activities should not be at the center of music education that tries to foster long-term musical engagement. Rather, the teacher should facilitate self-directed musical activities and learning, helping young people gain knowledge and skills they will need for the future. Lifelong musical engagement concerns every student, whether they later become professional musicians in a symphony orchestra, highly committed semiprofessional singers in a chamber choir, or enthusiastic members in a village brass band or just enjoy playing piano for themselves in their leisure time. Pitts states that if music education aims at supporting young people's lifelong musical activities, it has to combine "the structured imparting of skills and goals that is a feature of the best teaching, along with the modeling of valued leisure activities and open-minded cultural awareness."[64] Music education in schools has to empower students to be self-determined learners using the various kinds of musical creativities and resources available to them. This means that "one role of school music education must therefore be to ensure that all potential routes to future engagement are left open, so that the choices in lifelong participation lie with each individual, not with the limitations in his or her musical circumstances."[65] Young people should have the competencies to choose the musical path they enjoy most. They should feel empowered and be open-minded to explore differing kinds of musical activities, particularly in the communities they live in.[66] Connecting music education in schools with the respective communities students are a part of offers new perspectives on music and society, cultural diversity, and social justice. It emphasizes the social situatedness of music activities and the power music has for a community and individuals. Feeling the fascination of music in real-life settings, culture centers, community choirs or bands, and community theaters helps young people understand the transformative power of music for individuals and society. It can empower them to be a part of the ongoing and much-needed global process of transforming communities and society toward implementing social justice and cultural diversity, no matter what kind of musical engagement they choose, in formal or informal settings.

In recent years, informal learning has been a fascinating topic for music educators. It happens wherever people engage in music. It seems to exemplify a most natural way of learning, focused on listening, playing along, imitating, improvising, and trying out. No school environment, teacher, or structured curriculum is necessary. It is based on following one's own interests and musical passions, whether as a guitar player in a rock band or at the piano at home. Lucy Green identifies several important factors of informal learning in music that she uses for her classroom pedagogy.[67] First, informal learning begins with students choosing the music they like and would be interested to learn. This means that students are in charge of their own learning and decide what they will do. Second, the main method is listening and copying recordings by ear. Notation plays no role. If help is needed, a teacher can assist using different kinds of methods. Third, even though informal learning is self-directed, it can happen together with friends and peers. This often leads to negotiations as an important aspect of music making in bands, trying to find the best way to play a song. Fourth, informal learning is not well-structured sequential learning. Rather, informal learning practices tend to "be assimilated in haphazard, idiosyncratic and holistic ways, starting with 'whole,' 'real-world' pieces of music."[68] This means that informal learning can take more time than formal learning, following individual learning paths. Fifth, informal learning supports an integration of different musical activities such as listening, performing, improvising, or composing, thereby also fostering creativity. Even though the reproduction of a piece might be at the center of informal learning, learning through listening often leads to very individual versions of pieces, sometimes even cover versions of songs.

Using these five principles of informal learning for her classroom pedagogy, Green certainly supports the development of musical abilities facilitating lifelong musical engagement. Students today are often self-directed learners, having access to the information they need through recordings or electronic resources. They do not rely solely on the help of teachers anymore. But students need to acquire certain knowledge and skills to use informal learning practices effectively—for example, the ability to aurally identify musical structures and to be able to reproduce them on an instrument. Acquiring these skills supports the development of students' musicianship, because "such practices can change the ways pupils listen to, understand and appreciate music in and beyond the classroom."[69] However, it is important to point out that the way students learn informally is different from what a teacher would suggest. If students choose their own ways of learning, it might take longer, they might prefer detours, they might at some point need the advice of a teacher, or they might end up with a musical result different from that originally intended. But informal learning practices give students back the ownership of their learning processes. They connect the music classroom with individual musical worlds. In this way, music education becomes more meaningful for students, supporting them in their own musical journeys in a global world.

But despite all the benefits of informal learning, it is important to point out its limits, particularly regarding learning an instrument: Not all aspects can be covered by informal learning practices. It is often difficult to learn the right technique, posture, or expression through recordings or videos. This can lead to technical and musical deficits. Furthermore, students often learn only what they like, and musical activities are therefore "often restricted to the musical practice someone is acquainted with."[70] This can be a problem regarding the systematic development of musical skills, because it might stop at the point where a major effort is necessary to further develop the individual technique or musical expression. Therefore, from the perspective of instrumental pedagogy, Peter Mak argues for combining formal and informal learning strategies, understanding it as a "formal-informal continuum," supporting lifelong learning.[71] It is useful for young people to appreciate the benefits of informal learning practices but also to know when to turn to a teacher for musical guidance. This supports lifelong musical engagement, opens up new perspectives for musical learning, and helps redefine the role of the music teacher as a guide, adviser, and facilitator.

In view of globalization, it is important to note that the global music classroom is everywhere and that schools have to prepare their students for lifelong musical engagement. It is most comforting that people's musical engagement does not depend on music instruction and teachers, even though they can improve the enjoyment of music by supporting further skill development. The global music classroom, particularly regarding informal music practices, illustrates that everybody has something to teach to others and that places of musical engagement are most naturally places of musical learning. It does not matter if they exist in the real world or the virtual world of the internet. Everybody and everything is connected, thereby illustrating globalization and internationalization as thriving powers. Using the opportunities global music classrooms offer will be an important task for music education in the future, uniting musicians, music educators, and facilitators worldwide. The way the notion of the global music classroom is implemented in various countries can be a way of supporting globalizing music education. This is certainly connected with another conceptual element of the framework that this book presents: the global mindset.

Being Global

Different terms describe the kinds of intercultural knowledge, abilities, and skills that culturally sensitive people should have in today's diverse world. Global mindset, intercultural agility, cultural intelligence, international mindedness, or transcultural competence are just a few examples. While this terminological variety could seem overwhelming at first, it also has its benefits. It offers different perspectives on the same topic, depending on where the concepts originated (e.g., business studies) or the field of research on which it is based (e.g., psychology). These concepts can be easily applied to music education. The notions of global mindset, transcultural competence, and cultural agility could be particularly useful.

The Global Mindset

The global mindset is a model describing awareness and openness toward cultural diversity. It is a "psychological construct capturing a frame of reference based on interacting with people from geographically distant regions."[72] It tries to outline the knowledge and skills possessed by somebody who is able to successfully communicate and act in various cultures. It concerns having an open attitude, awareness of diversity, and curiosity, as well as acceptance of uncertainty and complexity. At the core of the global mindset is a filter through which we view the world. Everybody has a different filter, influenced by the past, individual experiences, expectations, and the culture he or she grew up in or encountered. While, in general, a mindset can be constructive or destructive (e.g., racist), the global mindset describes a positive filter, seeing the world in a specific way that values diversity. People who have a global mindset are open-minded and curious, willing to adjust their behavior to the various circumstances.[73] This openness can concern the professional or private life, thereby shaping somebody's personality. Research indicates that the global mindset has three elements, relating to psychological, social, and intellectual capital.[74] They indicate that a global mindset affects different parts of a personality. Psychological capital describes personal attributes such as curiosity, openness to new experiences, and cognitive flexibility. It enables people to enjoy experiencing various cultures, to have a variety of perspectives on situations, and to find creative solutions respecting the values of different cultural contexts. Intellectual capital refers to knowledge of various cultures, of globalization, of the different fields people work in, or of the rules they follow. Social capital describes the relationships and the networks people have, both professionally and personally. These networks have an immense value with regard to facilitating and supporting professional activities. They are important capital in a globally connected world. It is essential to know how to build and to foster such networks. Psychological, intellectual, and social capital indicate that the global mindset is complex and not easy to acquire. The most difficult dimension might be psychological capital, because it involves significant individual transformation. Appreciating diversity, being curious about and sensitive to various contexts, accepting contradictions, or paying attention to the interests of minorities is not easy to accomplish. It concerns interest in continuous improvement, for both oneself and others, including making necessary adjustments. Having a long-term point of view, not being focused on achieving short-term goals and quick successes, is also essential. This includes looking for opportunities in uncertainties and having faith in organizational processes, trusting coworkers, and not relying on tight control. Systemic thinking in the sense of identifying interdependencies and anticipating possible results and consequences of actions are part of a global mindset, too. When generally trying to characterize what the global mindset is, it most likely can be understood as a cosmopolitan perspective.[75] It represents a complex filter for interpreting the world in a cosmopolitan way. Asterios G. Kefalas summarizes:

> It is a filter through which we look at the world. A global mindset means that we scan the world from a broad perspective, always looking for unexpected trends and opportunities that may constitute a threat or an opportunity to achieve our personal, professional, or organizational objectives.[76]

The concept of the global mindset indicates what is most important in view of globalization and globalizing music education: to be culturally sensitive, flexible, comfortable with conflicts, and able to reconcile opposite positions. There are no simple solutions anymore. Being able to adapt to different situations is crucial in today's global world. This certainly concerns many professions and fields of research, including music education.

Most concepts of intercultural competencies such as the global mindset are based on research about culture and intercultural awareness, particularly that conducted by Edward Hall, Fons Trompenaars, or Geert Hofstede.[77] One of these concepts is transcultural competence. It concerns the "ability to successfully deal with and develop solutions to issues and problems created by cultural differences within any cultural setting" and is focused on difficulties caused by intercultural clashes and possible ways of reconciling them.[78] It is characterized by what Trompenaars calls the four Rs: recognition, respect, reconciliation, and realization.[79] They stand for a strategy that helps solve intercultural conflicts. First, the cultural dilemma is identified in terms of recognition. Second, the notion of respect accepts that differing opinions are possible and need to be acknowledged. Third, reconciliation describes finding an agreement and overcoming a cultural dilemma. Finally, the solution should result in action, thereby realizing and implementing the agreement found. The four Rs describe abilities culturally competent people have but also indicate the process of solving cultural dilemmas.

While transcultural competence seems to imply that solving intercultural dilemmas is a rather straightforward process, this might not always be the case, as the notion of cultural agility indicates. As meta-competency, it encompasses three levels: cultural adaptation, cultural minimization, and cultural integration.[80] They emphasize distinct ways of reacting to cultural differences in terms of transforming behavior according to the cultural context (adaptation), emphasizing one's own cultural values and norms despite the expectations of people from another culture (minimization), or finding a compromise that would honor other perspectives (integration). These aspects indicate nuanced reactions to cultural differences, going beyond oversimplified solutions such as tolerating everything or believing that everything will somehow work out. Cultural agility is a complex competency that involves overcoming cultural stereotypes and superficial assumptions about cross-cultural competencies but also cultural humility in terms of acknowledging a lifelong learning process.

These and many more concepts describe much-needed competencies regarding globalizing music education. The notion of global mindset indicates that becoming global means broadening common ways of thinking and acting. It involves becoming open minded and comfortable with ambiguity or cultural dilemmas. It means lifelong learning. Developing a global mindset concerns teachers and scholars, students and institutions. As individuals, each in our role, we have to accept that neither our personal and national perspectives on music education and research nor the international Anglo-American model is the only truth. Various cultures and traditions are legitimate parts of the international music education community and enrich it regarding being a diverse community. Self-reflection, both as a community and as individuals, can be a first step toward developing a global mindset. A starting point can be becoming aware of the variety of music education and research traditions, which research culture dominates the global discourse, and how much we sometimes long for easy solutions and international standards. Acknowledging diversity and being able to cope with it is important in view of globalization. The three types of capital the global mindset encompasses can be a useful orientation: We need to develop intellectual capital for acquiring knowledge about music education and research cultures. Psychological capital in terms of openness, curiosity, and having cognitive flexibility when getting in touch with new cultures is also crucial and involves a lifelong learning process. This particularly concerns being comfortable with ambiguity and having a long-term perspective instead of being focused on immediate success. In many situations where music educators and scholars from different countries meet, there are problems of communication regarding terms, scholarly concepts, or approaches. The way some write, give a presentation, or lead a discussion could also be different from what some other people might expect. Even on a personal level, there might be confusion or misunderstandings about the other person's reactions, teaching philosophies, or music education approaches. Knowing that these situations might happen and are a most natural part of international encounters helps avoid stress. Having the necessary intellectual and psychological capital supports solving cultural dilemmas in music education. Social capital in terms of being part of an international network is a particularly important aspect of being global. It helps get in touch with people from different music education cultures and research traditions and can be used as a training field for developing a global mindset.

International scholars, teachers, and students need to be committed to lifelong intercultural learning, acknowledging that making mistakes is part of developing a global mindset. While there are usually general intercultural training programs at universities, for the field of music education these programs would need to be adapted—for example, through research investigating distinct research cultures or different ways of scholarly writing in music education.[81] This would facilitate valuing the variety of music education and research cultures in which international students and scholars studying and working at universities worldwide have originally been socialized, thereby opening up a broader dialogue. The voices of students, teachers, and scholars from various music education and research traditions need to be heard. Their experiences in their home countries but also in a new and international environment are important, including all the processes in identity formation that take place.

For the future of the global music education community, it will be important to realize that the identity formation of scholars and teachers takes place partly within an international context. Developing a global mindset should be part of this process, for students, educators, and scholars living abroad, as well as for the teachers and advisers they encounter in their guest country. Developing a global mindset concerns not only people living in foreign countries. Because of international mobility and global migration, we have to deal with different cultures in our daily lives and to come to terms with them, no matter where we live. This includes encountering the unknown and maybe strange, being confused, or being unable to reconcile opposing positions. When encountering the unfamiliar, strange, or foreign, it is important to see it as such and not try to superficially deny differences. We tend to focus on either similarities or differences, minimizing or maximizing them while not sufficiently acknowledging the reality. It is essential to practice a realistic perspective, avoiding easy solutions that see things as completely different or alike. Eva Saether, Alagi Mbye, and Reza Shayestehe might be right when arguing for "breaking the equilibrium" in view of intercultural encounters:[82] Keeping the imbalance alive and acknowledging the differences between cultures supports a creative and transformative dialogue in intercultural encounters. It is important to realize that we are not all alike and that we do not need to be. It is not necessary to reconcile all cultural differences and dilemmas we encounter. Rather, embracing diversity and learning to understand each other can be enriching, be liberating, and facilitate much-needed transformative processes in music education globally and in individual lives.

Transforming Music Education

To address the challenges and opportunities globalization presents, music education has to change in terms of globalizing music education. The way we used to think and act is no longer appropriate. We need to reconsider and revise what music education is and intends and who we are as a global community. We need to think about what we can do to improve the impact music education has on our societies, toward supporting musical and individual development but also implementing social justice and inclusion and fostering cultural diversity. One of the main challenges might be to use music and music education not just for utilitarian and nonmusical goals. Music itself is powerful, and musical experiences have an impact on individual lives and personal growth. There is no need to use music only as a means for attaining nonmusical goals. Learning how to navigate between the aesthetic value of music as art and music as a means for nonmusical goals, such as creativity or intelligence, will be crucial for the future of music education in view of globalization.[83]

The call for transforming music education is not new. At various times, the need for transformation has been proclaimed. But even though we are familiar with changes and we might even be in the process of constant transformations, real change is not easy to accomplish. It affects our professional and personal identities and might disturb what we consider to be our most comfortable way of thinking and acting. Transformation challenges us as individuals and as a profession. It is a call to leave the common habits behind and look for new answers, taking into account the current challenges to create future directions and visions. Transformation in music education can, as Estelle Jorgensen points out, concern different aspects such as music, education, worldview, gender, tradition, or mindset.[84] We constantly have to revise and redefine our notions about these and other issues, depending on changing circumstances, conditions, and actors. Some of them might be easier to transform, others harder, such as individual mindsets. While initial steps in transformation might sometimes not seem too difficult— for example, changing the music featured in music classrooms—sustainable transformations are not easy to accomplish. The character of transformations can also differ, depending on the way they are introduced or the intentions that they have. Jorgensen points out different images that can illustrate processes of transformation, such as modification, accommodation, integration, assimilation, or renewal.[85] They indicate that there are different kinds of changes, some more smooth, others more sudden and radical, exemplifying various kinds of relationships between the old and the new state of affairs. Metaphors such as revolution

or transgression underline these aspects even more:[86] transformations can happen in a radical way, breaking with former ways of conduct, implementing new
worldviews or ideologies, with pressure and violence if needed. But it could also
be a smooth change, an ongoing process that is rarely noticed by anybody. The
success of transformations in music education certainly depends on the way they
are orchestrated and implemented by people involved or in charge. Images such
as revolution or transgression are useful to capture the nature of transformations
and to help people better understand what is going on or what their role might be.

In general, metaphors can function as intuitive guidelines for transformative
processes, summarizing the status quo or presenting visions for a better future.
They address our intuition and imagination, thereby engaging two of our most
effective powers when it comes to transformation. They help us understand in a
holistic way what we face in our daily music education practice and thus facilitate
imagining alternative ways of thinking and acting. Images such as music education as a boutique, the music teacher's job as a therapist, or the metaphors of fac-
tory and production challenge our sometimes hidden assumptions about music
teaching and learning.[87] They can concern our individual teaching philosophies
or issues of the entire profession, such as the images of village and community.
The village exemplifies a simple vision of music education, including close relationships, mutual support, self-governance, and democracy in contrast to community as a more complicated network of people and activities. Music education
as a community is focused more on the organization of learning, music as a social
practice, joint music making, and related stories and myths but also curricula
and administration. It usually involves many people. Community stands in Jorgensen's description for a multifaceted image of music education, involving different voices, approaches, and powers. The notion of community might imply
more openness regarding transformative processes, but the meaning of metaphors depends on the value individuals or a group of people give them. It is important to have a variety of images. Individuals can use them as illustrations for
their notions of music education, as a guide for transformations, or to create new
visions that match best their own notion of music education and transformation.

Transformation is certainly not an easy process for individuals and institutions. It is dialectical in nature and bound to the past, its values, and security but
also to the future and new visions. It often involves leaving behind well-known
models of thinking and acting that gave meaning to everyday work, moving toward an often-unknown future. Agreeing to the dynamic process of transformation, not knowing exactly how it might work out or how one's personal, professional, or institutional identity can be preserved within new circumstances, can
be challenging. Concepts in change management try to facilitate this process and
could also be applied to the field of music education.[88] This can help master the
challenges of transformations, both on a theoretical level—delivering a guiding

concept and a change of mindsets, policies, or organizations—and on a practical level with regard to implementation. It is important to listen to many voices and to include their opinions and suggestions for revisions, without losing sight of the goals of transformations. Jorgensen states:

> Music teachers need to help shape culture and the directions in which society moves. Teachers and educational policy makers cannot afford to remain passive or reactive. Nor should they leave the work of transformation to others. Rather, they need to commit to transforming education toward a humane and civil society. And given the nature of their subject matter, musicians and artists are especially positioned to create a powerful model of a humane and holistic music education that can help to transform education generally and those who undertake or undergo it.[89]

This is an ardent call for taking part in transformative processes and not leaving the power to political or administrative decision makers or stakeholders. Even if transformations challenge us and might be painful, we need to participate in them in order to shape music education in the way we want it to be. Realizing this fact is particularly important, because many people complain about transformations and administrative work. But when we are a part of it, we can change it and are responsible for it, at least to a certain degree. We do have power to transform music education, even if we often do not realize it.

But what exactly would transformation mean for music education today? Addressing globalization would certainly be a starting point, acknowledging the dialectics of diversity and unity within the international music education community. The UNESCO document *Rethinking Education: Towards a Global Common Good?* provides some interesting thoughts on transforming education that could be applied to music education.[90] Following the two landmark UNESCO publications *Learning to Be: The World of Education Today and Tomorrow* and *Learning: The Treasure Within*,[91] this newer document tries to rethink education in a changing world. Developed by a senior expert group, *Rethinking Education* was published in November 2015. It envisions a new path for education, addressing the changes caused by globalization and arguing for sustainable transformations in education internationally. The investigation is focused on four areas—namely, sustainable development, reaffirming a humanistic approach to education, education policy making in a complex world, and education as a common good. These perspectives approach the topic of transformation in education from several directions and can be applied to or supported by music education. The first section investigates sustainable development and argues for human rights as the general framework in education, implementing and protecting everybody's freedom and right to live a good and meaningful life. Music certainly plays an important role in a meaningful life—for example, as an expression of individual, communal, or cultural identity. Music education, community music, and also informal learning activities offer access to music making, thereby supporting cultural diversity and social justice, using music to raise awareness for the significance of cultural heritage and identity. According to *Rethinking Education*, valuing the diversity of worldviews and ways of knowing is important today, particularly in view of the advances in technology or neurosciences. These innovations interconnect the world more intensely and raise awareness for new approaches to knowledge and learning. The diversity of worldviews, including respect for religious and spiritual perspectives in indigenous cultures, not only supplements a Western European perspective based on Enlightenment ideas but is indispensable when addressing the challenges of globalization. This can concern broader justifications of human rights, whether based on general humanistic or Enlightenment ideas or related to spiritual or religious worldviews in terms of human beings being connected to nature, a heavenly order, or as an image of some god. Many worldviews emphasize respect for nature and every living being. When trying to support sustainable development through education, "alternative knowledge systems need to be recognized and properly accounted for, rather than relegated to an inferior status."[92] Valuing diverse ways of knowing also concerns the arts and music. Music can function as a specific type of knowledge beyond words, as proclaimed by authors of the romantic era or in Susanne Langer's notion of music as a symbol of emotional life.[93] Music can be an alternative way of gaining insights, thereby supporting transformational processes in individuals, communities, and societies. Embracing different kinds of knowledge, including insights and values transmitted through the arts, can help overcome the hegemony of a Western European worldview and its possible relatedness to issues of colonialism. Furthermore, education should be accessible to everybody and empower people to build "the human resources we need to be productive, to continue to learn, to solve problems, to be creative, and to live together and with nature in peace and harmony."[94] Education, including music education, can help support individual and communal development and offer a place for strengthening cultural identity.

Music education should be a vital part of every education system that aims at being transformative, trying to change or enrich mindsets and worldviews. It also concerns critical thinking and the ability to form self-determined and well-informed judgments, including the capability for discussions and debates. This enables individuals to be valuable members of a society, participating in democratic processes, supporting equal rights and social justice and thereby constantly helping improve society. Experiences as musicians, or members of an ensemble or informed aesthetic judgments and related discussions significantly support the development of critical thinking skills. They foster a humanistic approach to education that is guided by ethical principles supporting peace, inclusion, social justice, and environmental stewardship. Even though education and music education cannot solely solve socioeconomic problems, they can contribute significantly to mastering the challenges presented by globalization. A humanistic understanding points out that "education is not only about the acquisition of skills, it is also about values of respect for life and human dignity required for social harmony in a diverse world."[95] This can certainly be interpreted as a critique of neoliberal educational philosophies, which reduce education to the mere acquisition of skills and to a main factor in the economic and social advancement of nationstates. A humanistic approach to education respects human dignity and aims at being inclusive and accessible for everybody, embracing lifelong learning and the opportunities the internet and digital technology offer. Technology supports self-directed and nonformal learning, also leading to revisiting the role teachers and curriculum play. Music education can certainly make valuable contributions to a humanistic approach to education in terms of helping people develop their creativity and self-expression or share their cultural heritage. Diversity in music classrooms, music as a means for inclusive activities to take place, and reflecting music in culture and as culture can support this. Being human is deeply connected to being musical. Having access to music making is a basic human right.

But to implement a humanistic approach to education, changes in educational policy are necessary. When facing global challenges such as youth unemployment or the disconnection between formal education and the work world, we need an international educational policy framework facilitating the necessary changes.[96] This also concerns addressing problems of financing of the educational sector, in which many private parties are involved and often support the development of elite educational institutions. Challenges we face as a global community might even concern national educational systems and their intention to educate citizens who feel responsible for the public welfare in their own state but need to develop both national and global identities. Music education policy is part of general educational policy. Realizing that we are a global community can empower people to become engaged in music education policy, helping revise it toward implementing humanistic ideals and supporting sustainable development.

Reconsidering education in view of the challenges posed by globalization means understanding education to be a common good. The global community has to ensure that everybody has access to education. It is certainly a human right, but this concerns not only basic education but also secondary and postbasic education, including opportunities for lifelong learning. The understanding of education as a common good underlines that we are a global community, depending on each other to create a better future:

> The creation of knowledge as well as its acquisition, validation and use, are common to all people as part of a collective societal endeavor. . . . It emphasizes a participatory process in defining what a common good is which takes into account a diversity of contexts, concepts of well-being and knowledge ecosystems.[97]

In an interconnected world, we need to value the diversity of knowledges. Education and knowledge need to be related to our global concerns, offering paths for individual development and supporting the welfare of our global community. Music education is a significant part of education, individual lives, and happiness. It is related to formal and nonformal education and exemplifies our shared knowledge and cultural heritage, celebrating diversity and supporting people in their individual life journeys. Music and music education are therefore part of the notion of education as a common good and need to be included when considering a humanistic and sustainable vision for education in today's world.

Implementing the transformations the UNESCO document suggests would be a first step toward addressing the challenges posed by globalization and internationalization. They certainly require such changes and the development of a vision for music education toward humane ends, based on ethical principles and embracing diversity. But transformations are dialectical, related to both the past and the present, depending on the ability of individuals to balance these dimensions. Transformations are never without problems, often connected to fears and resistance. To facilitate transitions, these problems need to be addressed. Developing a global mindset in particular is not an easy task. It is necessary for survival not only in foreign countries but also for domestic endeavors, because we encounter cultural diversity everywhere. Therefore, individuals and institutions should embrace transformation, even though real change might take a long time. Music and music education can be starting points for the much-needed transformations in education and societies, and everybody can be a part of this, because being musical is part of what it means to be human. The conceptual framework presented in this book can help facilitate this process and inspire future research, supporting the implementation of a unified and diverse global music education community. This is what globalizing music education means.

Notes

1. Patrick M. Jones, "Why We Need Policy Research in Music Education and What We Can Do to Create an Impactful Policy Community in and for Music Education," in *Policy and Media in and for a Diverse Global Community*, ed. Peter Gouzouasis (Vancouver: University of British Columbia, 2014), 85, http://issuu.com/official_isme/docs/2014_isme_policy_procedings/1?e=1871 006/8519907.

2. Anne Larason Schneider and Helen Ingram, *Policy Design for Democracy* (Lawrence: University Press of Kansas, 1997), 2.

3. Patrick Schmidt, "Cosmopolitanism and Policy: A Pedagogical Framework for Global Issues in Music Education," *Arts Education Policy Review* 114 (2013): 103.

4. Patrick Schmidt, "Why Policy Matters: Developing a Policy Vocabulary within Music Education," in *Policy and the Political Life of Music Education*, ed. Patrick Schmidt and Richard Colwell (New York: Oxford University Press, 2017), 12.

5. Jones, "Why We Need Policy Research in Music Education," 86.

6. Ibid., 85.

7. Ibid., 88.

8. Marie McCarthy, "International Perspectives," in *The Oxford Handbook of Music Education*, ed. Gary E. McPherson and Graham F. Welch (New York: Oxford University Press, 2012), 1:42–54.

9. Ibid., 57.

10. Ibid.

11. Ibid., 41.

12. For more information, see the website of the ISME Commission on Policy: Culture, Education and Media, at https://www.isme.org/our-work/commissions-forum/commission-policy-culture-education-and-media.

13. For more information, see the council's website, at http://www.musikrat.de.

14. For more information, see the association's website, at http://www.nafme.org.

15. Michael L. Mark and Patrice Madura, *Contemporary Music Education* (London: Wadsworth, 2013), 69.

16. Hans Guenther Bastian, *Musik(erziehung) und ihre Wirkung: Eine Langzeitstudie an Berliner Grundschulen* [Music (education) and its impact: A long-term study at elementary schools in Berlin] (Mainz, Germany: Schott, 2000).

17. See Don Campbell, *The Mozart Effect: Tapping the Power of Music to Heal the Body, Strengthen the Mind, and Unlock the Creative Spirit* (New York: Avon Books, 1997).

18. Hildegard Froehlich, *A Social Theory for Music Education* (Lewiston, NY: Edwin Mellen Press, 2015), 167.

19. Ibid., 169–176.

20. Ibid., 171.

21. Ibid.

22. Ibid., 173.

23. Ibid., 174.

24. Ibid., 175.

25. Michael Fullan and Suzanne M. Stiegelbauer, *The New Meaning of Educational Change*, 2nd ed. (London: Cassell, 1996), 65.

26. Chi Cheung Leung, "A Theoretical Framework on Effective Implementation of Music/Arts Education Policy in Schools," in *Music Education Policy and Implementation: International Perspectives*, ed. Chi Cheung Leung, Lai Chi Rita Yip, and Tadahiko Imada (Hirosaki, Japan: Hirosaki University Press, 2008), 8.

27. Ibid., 11–15.

28. Ibid., 11.

29. Liane Hentschke, "Global Policies and Local Needs of Music Education in Brazil," *Arts Education Policy Review* 114 (2013): 120–123.

30. Ibid., 122.

31. Ibid., 123.

32. Ibid., 121.

33. United Nations Educational, Scientific and Cultural Organization, "Road Map for Arts Education," 2006, http://www.unesco.org/new/fileadmin/MULTIMEDIA/HQ/CLT/CLT/pdf/Arts_Edu_RoadMap_en.pdf. See also Anne Bamford, *The Wow Factor: Global Research Compendium on the Impact of the Arts in Education* (Münster, Germany: Waxmann, 2006).

34. Anne Bamford, "Making It Happen: Closing the Gap between Policy and Practice in Arts Education," in *The Routledge International Handbook of the Arts and Education*, ed. Mike Fleming, Liora Bresler, and John O'Toole (New York: Routledge, 2015), 396.

35. For more information, see Lucy Green, *Learning, Teaching and Musical Identity* (Bloomington: Indiana University Press, 2011); and Lucy Green, *How Popular Musicians Learn: A Way Ahead of Music Education* (Aldershot, UK: Ashgate, 2001).

36. Pamela Burnard, *Musical Creativities in Practices* (New York: Oxford University Press, 2012).

37. Allison James and Adrian James, *Key Concepts in Childhood Studies* (London: Sage, 2012), 64–65.

38. United Nations, "Convention on the Rights of the Child," November 20, 1989, http://www.ohchr.org/EN/ProfessionalInterest/Pages/CRC.aspx.

39. Marilyn Fleer, Marianne Hedegaard, and Jonathan Tudge, *Childhood Studies and the Impact of Globalization: Policies and Practices at Global and Local Levels* (London: Routledge, 2009), 5.

40. Bame Nsamenang, "Cultures in Early Childhood Care and Education," in *Childhood Studies and the Impact of Globalization: Policies and Practices at the Global and Local Levels*, ed. Marilyn Fleer, Marianne Hedegaard, and Jonathan Tudge (London: Routledge, 2009), 24.

41. Karen Wells, *Childhood in a Global Perspective* (Cambridge, UK: Polity 1999), 4.

42. Alexandra Kertz-Welzel, "Transcultural Childhoods," in *The Child as Musician*, 2nd ed., ed. Gary E. McPherson (Oxford: Oxford University Press, 2016), 577–593.

43. Patricia Shehan Campbell and Trevor Wiggins, "Giving Voices to Children," in *The Oxford Handbook of Children's Musical Cultures*, ed. Patricia Shehan Campbell and Trevor Wiggins (Oxford: Oxford University Press, 2013), 7.

44. Robert Pitzer, "Youth Music at the Yakama Tribal School," in Campbell and Wiggins, *The Oxford Handbook of Children's Musical Cultures*, 46–60.

45. Sally Bodkin-Allen, "Interweaving Threads of Music in the Whariki of Early Childhood Cultures in Aotearoa/New Zealand," in Campbell and Wiggins, *The Oxford Handbook of Children's Musical Cultures*, 387–401.

46. Lily Chen-Hafteck, "Balancing Change and Tradition in the Musical Lives of Children in Hong Kong," in Campbell and Wiggins, *The Oxford Handbook of Children's Musical Cultures*, 402–418.

47. Patricia Shehan Campbell and Trevor Wiggins, "Giving Voices to Children," in Campbell and Wiggins, *The Oxford Handbook of Children's Musical Cultures*, 3.

48. Kathryn Marsh, *The Musical Playground: Global Tradition and Changes in Children's Songs and Games* (New York: Oxford University Press, 2008).

49. Wolfgang Welsch, "Transculturality—the Puzzling Form of Cultures Today," in *Spaces of Culture: City, Nation, World*, ed. Mike Featherstone and Scott Lash (London: Sage 1999), 194–213, http://www2.uni-jena.de/welsch/papers/W_Wlelsch_Transculturality.html.

50. Alexandra Kertz-Welzel, "Transcultural Childhoods," 594.

51. For more information, see the website of Wolfgang Martin Stroh, Multicultural Music Education in Germany, at http://www.interkulturelle-musikerziehung.de/multicultural_me/index.html.

52. Irmgard Merkt, *Deutsch-tuerkische Musikpaedagogik in der Bundesrepublik: ein Situationsbericht* [German-Turkish music education in Germany: A situation report] (Essen, Germany: Express Edition, 1983).

53. Alexandra Kertz-Welzel, "Multicultural or Intercultural? The Impact of Political Conceptions on Music Education Approaches in Germany and the United States," paper presented at the 8th International RIME (Research in Music Education) Conference, Exeter, UK, April 9–13, 2013.

54. Patricia Shehan Campbell, *Teaching Music Globally* (New York: Oxford University Press, 2004), 54–213.

55. Ibid., 126.

56. Ibid.

57. Deborah Bradley, "Music Education, Multiculturalism, and Anti-racism—Can We Talk?" *Action, Criticism and Theory for Music Education* 5, no. 2 (2006), http://act.mayday group.org/articles/Bradley5_2.pdf.

58. Juliet Hess, "Performing Tolerance and Curriculum: The Politics of Self-Congratulation, Identity Formation, and Pedagogy in World Music Education," *Philosophy of Music Education Review* 21, no. 1 (2013): 66–91.

59. Tia DeNora, *Music in Everyday Life* (Cambridge: Cambridge University Press, 2000); Tia DeNora, *Music Asylums: Wellbeing through Music in Everyday Life* (Farnham, UK: Ashgate, 2013).

60. Burnard, *Musical Creativities in Practices*, 228.

61. John Finney and Pamela Burnard, *Music Education with Digital Technology* (London: Continuum, 2007).

62. Stephanie E. Pitts, "Fostering Lifelong Engagement in Music," in *The Child as Musician*, 2nd ed., ed. Gary E. McPherson (Oxford: Oxford University Press, 2016), 639.

63. David E. Myers, "Freeing Music Education from Schooling: Toward a Lifespan Perspective on Music Learning and Teaching," *International Journal of Community Music* 1, no. 1 (2007), http://www.intellectbooks.co.uk/MediaManager/Archive/IJCM/Volume%20D/03%20 Myers.pdf.

64. Pitts, "Fostering Lifelong Engagement in Music," 651.

65. Stephanie E. Pitts, *Chances and Choices: Exploring the Impact of Music Education* (New York: Oxford University Press, 2012), 173.

66. Patrick M. Jones, "Returning Music Education to the Mainstream: Reconnecting with the Community," *Visions of Research in Music Education* 7 (January 2006), http://www-usr .rider.edu/~vrme/v7n1/visions/Jones%20Returning%20Music%20Education%20to%20 the%20Mainstream.pdf.

67. Lucy Green, *Music, Informal Learning and the School: A New Classroom Pedagogy* (Farnham, UK: Ashgate, 2009), 10.

68. Ibid.

69. Ibid., 2.

70. Peter Mak, "Formal, Non-formal and Informal Learning in Music," in *Vom wilden Lernen* [About wild learning], ed. Peter Roebke and Natalie Ardilla-Mantilla (Mainz, Germany: Schott, 2009), 39.

71. Ibid., 40.

72. P. Christopher Earley, Charles Murnieks, and Elaine Mosakowski, "Cultural Intelligence and the Global Mindset," in *The Global Mindset*, ed. Mansour Javidan, Richard M. Steers, and Michael A. Hitt (Oxford: JAI Elsevier, 2007), 79.

73. Kalburgi M. Srinivas, "Globalization of Business and the Third World," *Journal of Management Development* 14, no. 3 (1995): 30.

74. Rachel Clapp-Smith, Fred Luthans, and Bruce J. Avolio, "The Role of Psychological Capital in Global Mindset Development," in Javidan, Steers, and Hitt, *The Global Mindset*, 105–130.

75. Earley, Murnieks, and Mosakowski, "Cultural Intelligence and the Global Mindset," 80.

76. Asterios G. Kefalas, "Think Globally, Act Locally," *Thunderbird International Business Review* 40, no. 6 (1998): 556.

77. Geert Hofstede, *Culture's Consequences: Comparing Values, Behaviours, Institutions and Organizations across Nations* (London: Sage, 2003); Geert Hofstede, Gert Jan Hofstede, and Michael Minkov, *Cultures and Organizations: Software of the Mind* (New York: McGraw-Hill,

2004); Fons Trompenaars and Charles Hampden-Turner, *Riding the Waves of Culture: Understanding Diversity in Global Business* (New York: McGraw-Hill, 1998); Edward T. Hall, *Beyond Culture* (Garden City, NY: Anchor Press, 1976).

78. Jerry Glover and Harris L. Friedman, *Transcultural Competence: Navigating Cultural Differences in the Global Community* (Washington, DC: American Psychological Association, 2015), 8.

79. Ibid., 8–9.

80. Paula Caliguiri, *Cultural Agility: Building a Pipeline of Successful Global Professionals* (San Francisco: Jossey-Bass, 2012), 5.

81. Sandra M. Fowler and Judith M. Blohm, "An Analysis for Methods of Intercultural Training," in *Handbook of Intercultural Training*, ed. Dan Landis, Janet M. Bennett, and Milton J. Bennett (London: Sage, 2004), 37–84.

82. Eva Saether, Alagi Mbye, and Reza Shayestehe, "Intercultural Tensions and Creativity in Music," in *The Oxford Handbook of Music Education*, ed. Gary E. McPherson and Graham F. Welsh (New York: Oxford University Press, 2012), 2:367.

83. The northern European concept of *Bildung* in music is a useful approach for reconciling musical and nonmusical goals. See Alexandra Kertz-Welzel, "Revisiting Bildung and Its Meaning for International Music Education Policy," in *Policy and the Political Life of Music Education*, ed. Patrick Schmidt and Richard Colwell (New York: Oxford University Press, 2017), 107–121.

84. Estelle R. Jorgensen, *Transforming Music Education* (Bloomington: Indiana University Press, 2003), 19–47.

85. Ibid., 48–76.

86. Estelle R. Jorgensen, *Pictures of Music Education* (Bloomington: Indiana University Press, 2011).

87. Ibid.

88. Rixa Regina Kroehl, *Change Management* (Konstanz, Germany: UVK, 2016).

89. Jorgensen, *Transforming Music Education*, xii.

90. United Nations Educational, Scientific, and Cultural Organization, *Rethinking Education: Towards a Global Common Good?* (Paris: UNESCO, 2015), http://unesdoc.unesco.org /images/0023/002325/232555e.pdf.

91. Edgar Faure, Filipe Herrera, Abdul-Razzak Kaddoura, Henri Lopes, Arthur V. Petrovsky, Majid Rahnema, and Frederick Champion Ward, *Learning to Be: The World of Education Today and Tomorrow* (Paris: UNESCO, 1972), http://unesdoc.unesco.org/images /0000/000018/001801e.pdf; International Commission on Education for the Twenty-First Century, *Learning: The Treasure Within* (Paris: UNESCO, 1996), http://unesdoc.unesco.org /images/0010/001095/109590eo.pdf.

92. Ibid., 30.

93. Susanne K. Langer, *Philosophy in a New Key* (New York: New American Library, 1957).

94. Ibid., 32.

95. Ibid., 37.

96. Ibid., 59.

97. Ibid., 11.

Conclusion

THIS BOOK PROPOSES the vision of a united yet diverse and culturally sensitive global music education community. For addressing the challenges that we face today, we need to unite our efforts and use the strengths we have as a multifaceted global community. This is what globalizing music education means. But globalizing music education is not something that can be done easily. Rather, this is a call for transforming music education. By acknowledging the many music education and research cultures, the notion of globalizing music education challenges the current state of music education worldwide—for instance, the so-far unquestioned hegemony of Anglo-American music education.

This book attempts to raise awareness for shaping international music education in a culturally sensitive way, trying to empower everybody who is interested to be a part of it. It presents a critical yet positive vision of music education, trying to overcome idealistic and simplified notions of globalization and internationalization. But it does not attempt to offer a comprehensive description of music education or research traditions in different countries. Rather, this book provides a conceptual framework, suggesting a theoretical structure of categories and conceptual elements that could facilitate globalizing music education. It breaks down the impact of globalization and internationalization on music education in selective categories presented in its chapters. At the same time, through these categories, it develops the notion of what globalizing music education could mean.

The framework presented in this book can be a tool for understanding, evaluating, and shaping globalizing music education in a culturally sensitive way. Through providing such a conceptual framework, this book also contributes to the methodology of comparative and international music education. However, when considering the global music education community, it is important to point out that, no matter what unites us, there are also differences. We should acknowledge and not ignore them. They are a significant part of who we are as a vivid, diverse, and creative global community. Keeping the imbalance alive regarding appreciating that we are similar but also different helps remind us that international encounters are always intercultural encounters, no matter how uniform we seem to be. Acknowledging that we need intercultural knowledge and competencies can facilitate a creative and transformative international dialogue, supporting the further formation of an inclusive and diverse global community.

Developing a global mindset is therefore an important prerequisite for mastering the challenges related to diversity in music education worldwide.

If we take globalization and internationalization seriously, we must reconsider the goals of music education and research. Universities and schools worldwide need to adjust to the new conditions. This will lead to changes in music teacher education programs and music education policy.[1] Preparing students to be lifelong musicians and learners will be a significant part of our task as a global music education community. Balancing musical and nonmusical goals will also be important for successful music education today. Being open to diversity and inclusion, no matter if embracing a variety of cultures, ethnicities, or abilities, enriches music education internationally. This particularly concerns trying to overcome the dominance of Western narratives in music teaching and research. This is what globalizing music education means.

These aspects indicate that, in view of globalization and internationalization, new visions for music education are indeed needed. Various publications have recently proposed important aspects of such visions for music education, emphasizing social justice,[2] inclusion,[3] or transformative music education.[4] Arguing for an open music education philosophy[5] or artistic citizenship[6] has also been presented as a new approach to addressing the challenges we face. Even though these are only a few visions among many more in the global community, they indicate what will be paramount for music education in the twenty-first century: the hope that music education can help transform individuals and societies toward implementing ideals of social justice, equality, diversity, and inclusiveness. While these are not new ideas, they seem to express the current longing of our profession to reconnect music education with the society. Certainly, these visions are not unproblematic. They are in danger of becoming oversimplified dreams of changing the world through music education, thereby being close to past misuses of music education for ideological purposes (e.g., during the Third Reich in Germany) or using music education as a means for utilitarian goals.[7] Visions need to be constantly revisited and challenged and also critically elaborated in view of the history of music education internationally. But they represent our current notions of music education and need to be considered when thinking about transforming music education and addressing the challenges and opportunities that globalization and internationalization represent.

When looking for a way of developing visions of music education toward humane ends, UNESCO's *Rethinking Education: Towards a Global Common Good?* can serve as a guideline. It presents a humanistic approach to education that is situated within the framework of human rights. Only when guided by ethical principles can education serve humane ends and help address the challenges of globalization and internationalization. However, educational policy making needs to consider that we live in a complex world where simple solutions no longer fit. Not only talking about human rights and ethical principles but finding ways to implement them in international education and music education policy will not be easy. Smart and flexible solutions are needed that acknowledge the differences in international education and music education but also the underlying ideas and ethical principles. This could result in creating a global humanistic approach in music education, one considering educational ideals of various educational and philosophical traditions.[8] But above all, it includes implementing education and music education as a common good by offering access for everybody. While technology certainly facilitates lifelong learning, the political framework should change, too. We need music educators and scholars active in music education policy, familiar with the processes in this field. But we also need research to prove the significance of music and music education, without always referring to superficial nonmusical benefits. Emphasizing the variety of ways that music and music education have a positive impact on people's lives, without marginalizing musical learning and intense musical experiences for their own sake, will be an important research task. Different kinds of musical activities, experiences, and learning facilitate the transformative power of music in the lives of individuals and for society.

A variety of visions in music education can help implement music education for humane ends and as a common good. But it is also necessary to keep in mind that education and music education cannot solve socioeconomic problems. We must be critically aware of the limits that new visions for music education have and the need to constantly revise and elaborate them. Likewise, this includes addressing developments that try to stop globalizing music education in favor of seclusion and a focus on national music, music education, or research cultures. This tendency challenges not only our societies but also the identity of our profession, which is based on understanding music as an expression of cultural identity and diversity. In the future, it will be a significant task for music educators and scholars globally to point out the value of diversity and internationalization in modern societies within the framework of human rights and aiming toward implementing social justice, equality, and inclusion.

Regarding music education as a field of research, comparative and international music education will play paramount roles. They can function as foundations for music education worldwide, broadening the national perspectives to international and global ones. Through research, both fields raise awareness for the diversity of music education and research traditions around the globe, supporting the knowledge that we are a global community, depending on each other to master the challenges ahead. Many topics we investigate are global concerns. Joining forces will help address more effectively global challenges, particularly owing to the richness of our different perspectives. But comparative and international music education also should address what links us as a global community in terms of international exchange processes such as educational transfer. Critically analyzing past processes and developing models for new exchanges can help overcome the unconscious and often ineffective copying of practices and policies. Similarly, we need to reconsider critically the global knowledge production in music education and the impact of geographical, geolinguistic, or geopolitical factors. This will be vital for globalizing music education. The concept of the global mindset, exemplifying a much-needed transformation of thinking toward international mindedness, could serve as a useful orientation in music education worldwide.

To shape the global music education community in a culturally sensitive way, it will be paramount to reconsider globalization and internationalization regarding sustaining local, regional, or national research cultures, languages, terminology, and publications, as well as global and international ones. A culturally sensitive global research culture and transcultural music education terminology, consisting of concepts and terms from various music education cultures, while still using English as the international language, could help acknowledge diversity and thereby enrich music education worldwide. Athelstan Canagarajah states:

> It is possible to develop a pluralistic mode of thinking where we celebrate different cultures and identities, and yet engage in projects common to our shared humanity. Breaking away from the history of constructing a globalized totality with uniform knowledge and hierarchical community, we should envision building a network of multiple centers that develop diversity as a universal project and encourage an actively negotiated epistemological tradition.[9]

This is an ardent call for developing new visions for music education globally. It is possible to embrace the diversity of cultures in music education and research worldwide while at the same time pursuing activities that underline what unites us. This means overcoming the illusion of being able to construct "a globalized totality with uniform knowledge and hierarchical community," reducing the variety of knowledges, worldviews, and power relations to a single truth. Instead, for globalizing music education in a way that supports diversity, particularly regarding scholarly cultures, this means creating a "network of multiple centers." It could consist of groups of music education scholars in countries representing certain research traditions. They could develop ideas regarding how implementing diversity in global music education and research could look, while at the same time underlining what unites us. Through research, these groups would try to find ways of respecting, negotiating, and using different epistemological, scholarly, and educational traditions in music education. Ultimately, this could lead to a more diverse global community using various kinds of knowledges and experiences to master the challenges we face. A network of multiple research centers conducting projects and facilitating international exchange and collaboration regarding diversity could be an important step toward improving music education and research globally.

Globalizing music education by developing a united yet diverse and culturally sensitive worldwide music education community is certainly no easy endeavor. But for the future of music education, this will be indispensable. This book offers a first step toward this important goal by providing a conceptual framework. Future research will have to apply and elaborate on this framework. If this book serves as a starting point for future research, then it will have accomplished its mission.

Notes

1. For suggestions for transforming higher education, see Edward Sarath, David Myers, and Patricia Shehan Campbell, *Redefining Music Studies in an Age of Change: Creativity, Diversity, Integration* (New York: Routledge, 2017).

2. Cathy Benedict, Patrick Schmidt, Gary Spruce, and Paul G. Woodford, *The Oxford Handbook of Social Justice in Music Education* (New York: Oxford University Press, 2015).

3. Judith A. Jellison, *Including Everyone: Creating Music Classrooms Where All Children Learn* (New York: Oxford University Press, 2015).

4. David J. Elliott and Marissa Silverman, *Music Matters: A Philosophy of Music Education* (New York: Oxford University Press, 2014).

5. Randall Everett Allsup, *Remixing the Classroom: Toward an Open Philosophy of Music Education* (Bloomington: Indiana University Press, 2016).

6. David J. Elliott, Marissa Silverman, and Wayne D. Bowman, *Artistic Citizenship: Artistry, Social Responsibility and Ethical Praxis* (New York: Oxford University Press, 2016).

7. Alexandra Kertz-Welzel, "The Pied Piper of Hamelin: Adorno on Music Education," *Research Studies in Music Education* 25, no. 1 (2005): 1–12.

8. Penny Enslin and Kai Horsthemke, "Can *Ubuntu* Provide a Model for Citizenship Education in African Democracies?," *Comparative Education* 40, no. 4 (2004): 545–558; Charlene Tan and Leonard Tan, "A Shared Vision of Human Excellence: Confucian Spirituality and Arts Education," *Pastoral Care in Education* 34, no. 3 (2016): 156–166.

9. Athelstan Suresh Canagarajah, "Reconstructing Local Knowledge, Reconfiguring Language Studies," in *Reclaiming the Local in Language, Policy and Practice*, ed. Athelstan Suresh Canagarajah (Mahwah, NJ: Lawrence Erlbaum, 2005), 20.

Bibliography

Adams, John. "Proposal for an American Language Academy." In *Language Loyalties: A Sourcebook on the Official English Controversy*, edited by James Crawford, 31–33. Chicago: University of Chicago Press, 1992.

Adick, Christel. "The Impact of Globalization on National Educational Systems." In *Globalisierung als Herausforderung der Erziehung* [Globalization as a challenge to education], edited by Christoph Wulf and Christine Merkel, 45–58. Münster, Germany: Waxmann, 2002.

Allsup, Randall Everett. *Remixing the Classroom: Toward an Open Philosophy of Music Education*. Bloomington: Indiana University Press, 2016.

American Council on Education. "CIGE Model for Comprehensive Internationalization." http://www.acenet.edu/news-room/Pages/CIGE-Model-for-Comprehensive-Internationalization.aspx (accessed June 28, 2017).

Anderson, Benedict. *Imagined Communities*. London: Verso, 2006.

Appadurai, Arjun. *Modernity at Large: Cultural Dimensions of Globalization*. Minneapolis: University of Minnesota Press, 1996.

Applegate, Celia, and Pamela Potter. "Germans as the 'People of Music': Genealogy of an Identity." In *Music and German National Identity*, edited by Celia Applegate and Pamela Potter, 1–35. Chicago: University of Chicago Press, 2002.

Arbeitskreis Deutsch als Wissenschaftssprache. "Guidelines." May 2015. http://www.adawis.de/admin/upload/navigation/data/Leitlinien%202015%20englisch.pdf.

Baker, Geoffrey. "Editorial Introduction: El Sistema in Critical Perspective." *Action, Criticism and Theory for Music Education* 15, no. 1 (2016): 10–32. http://act.maydaygroup.org/articles/Baker15_1.pdf.

Bamford, Anne. "Making It Happen: Closing the Gap between Policy and Practice in Arts Education." In *The Routledge International Handbook of the Arts and Education*, edited by Mike Fleming, Liora Bresler, and John O'Toole, 388–397. New York: Routledge, 2015.

———. *The Wow Factor: Global Research Compendium on the Impact of the Arts in Education*. Münster, Germany: Waxmann, 2006.

Bastian, Hans Guenther. *Musik(erziehung) und ihre Wirkung: Eine Langzeitstudie an Berliner Grundschulen* [Music (education) and its impact: A long-term study at elementary schools in Germany]. Mainz, Germany: Schott, 2000.

Becher, Tony. *Academic Tribes and Territories: Intellectual Enquiry and the Cultures of Disciplines*. Bristol, UK: Open University Press, 1989.

Benedict, Cathy, Patrick Schmidt, Gary Spruce, and Paul Woodford. *The Oxford Handbook of Social Justice in Music Education*. New York: Oxford University Press, 2015.

Bereday, George Z. F. *Comparative Method in Education*. New York: Holt, Rinehart, and Winston, 1964.

Bermann, Sandra. *A Companion to Translation Studies*. Chichester, UK: Wiley-Blackwell, 2014.

Bodkin-Allen, Sally. "Interweaving Threads of Music in the Whariki of Early Childhood Cultures in Aotearoa/New Zealand." In *The Oxford Handbook of Children's Musical Cultures*, edited by Patricia Shehan Campbell and Trevor Wiggins, 387–401. Oxford: Oxford University Press, 2013.

Bowman, Wayne. "Who Is the 'We'? Rethinking Professionalism in Music Education." *Action, Criticism and Theory for Music Education* 6, no. 4 (2007): 109–131. http://act .maydaygroup.org/articles/Bowman6_4.pdf.

Bradley, Deborah. "Music Education, Multiculturalism, and Anti-racism—Can We Talk?" *Action, Criticism and Theory for Music Education* 5, no. 2 (2006): 2–30. http:// act.maydaygroup.org/articles/Bradley5_2.pdf.

Brandenburg, Uwe, and Hans de Wit. "The End of Internationalization." *International Higher Education*, no. 62 (2011): 15–17. http://www.che.de/downloads/IHE_no_62 _Winter_2011.pdf.

Bray, Mark. *Comparative Education: Continuing Traditions, New Challenges, and New Paradigms*. Dordrecht, Netherlands: Kluwer, 2003.

Bray, Mark, Bob Adamson, and Mark Mason. *Comparative Education Research: Approaches and Methods*. Hong Kong: Springer, 2007.

Bray, Mark, and Murray R. Thomas. "Levels of Comparison in Educational Studies: Different Insights from Different Literatures and the Value of Multilevel Analysis." *Harvard Educational Review* 65, no. 3 (1995): 472–491.

Burnard, Pamela. *Musical Creativities in Practices*. New York: Oxford University Press, 2012.

Caliguiri, Paula. *Cultural Agility: Building a Pipeline of Successful Global Professionals*. San Francisco: Jossey-Bass, 2012.

Campbell, Don. *The Mozart Effect: Tapping the Power of Music to Heal the Body, Strengthen the Mind and Unlock the Creative Spirit*. New York: Avon Books, 1997.

Campbell, Patricia Shehan. *Lessons from the World*. London: Schirmer, 1991.

———. *Songs in Their Heads: Music and Its Meaning in Children's Lives*. 2nd ed. New York: Oxford University Press, 2010.

———. *Teaching Music Globally*. New York: Oxford University Press, 2004.

Campbell, Patricia Shehan, and Trevor Wiggins. "Giving Voices to Children." In *The Oxford Handbook of Children's Musical Cultures*, edited by Patricia Shehan Campbell and Trevor Wiggins, 1–24. Oxford: Oxford University Press, 2013.

———. *The Oxford Handbook of Children's Musical Cultures*. Oxford: Oxford University Press, 2013.

Canagarajah, Athelstan Suresh. "Reconstructing Local Knowledge, Reconfiguring Language Studies." In *Reclaiming the Local in Language, Policy and Practice*, edited by Athelstan Suresh Canagarajah, 3–24. Mahwah, NJ: Lawrence Erlbaum, 2005.

Carney, Stephen. "Negotiating Policy in an Age of Globalization: Exploring Educational 'Policyscapes' in Denmark, Nepal, and China." *Comparative Education Review* 53, no. 1 (2009): 63–88.

Cheng, Kai-Ming. "The Postindustrial Workplace and Challenges to Education." In *Learning in the Global Era*, edited by Marcelo M. Suarez-Orozco, 175–191. Berkeley: University of California Press, 2007.

Chen-Hafteck, Lily. "Balancing Change and Tradition in the Musical Lives of Children in Hong Kong." In *The Oxford Handbook of Children's Musical Cultures*, edited by

Patricia Shehan Campbell and Trevor Wiggins, 402–418. Oxford: Oxford University Press, 2013.

Clapp-Smith, Rachel, Fred Luthans, and Bruce J. Avolio. "The Role of Psychological Capital in Global Mindset Development." In *The Global Mindset*, edited by Mansour Javidan, Richard M. Steers, and Michael A. Hitt, 105–130. Oxford: JAI Elsevier, 2007.

Clark, Burton R. "Academic Culture." Working paper no. 42, Yale University Higher Education Research Group, 1980.

Clausen, Bernd. *Der Hase im Mond: Studie zu japanischer Musik im japanischen Musikunterricht* [The hare in the moon: A survey of Japanese music in Japanese music lessons]. Berlin: LIT, 2009.

Coupland, Nikolas. "Introduction." In *The Handbook of Language and Globalization*, edited by Nikolas Coupland, 1–28. Malden, MA: Wiley-Blackwell, 2010.

Cowen, Robert. "Comparing Futures or Comparing Pasts?" *Comparative Education* 36, no. 3 (2000): 333–342.

Cox, Gordon, and Robin Stevens. *The Origins and Foundations of Music Education*. London: Continuum, 2010.

———. *The Origins and Foundations of Music Education*. 2nd ed. London: Continuum, 2017.

Crystal, David. *English as a Global Language*. 2nd ed. Cambridge: Cambridge University Press 2003.

Dale, Roger, and Susan L. Robertson. "Towards a Critical Grammar of Education Policy Movement." In *World Yearbook of Education 2012: Policy Borrowing and Lending in Education*, edited by Gita Steiner-Khamsi and Florian Waldow, 21–40. New York: Routledge, 2012.

Daly, Herman E. "Globalization versus Internationalization." *Global Policy Forum*, 1999. https://www.globalpolicy.org/component/content/article/162/27995.html.

DeNora, Tia. *Music Asylums: Wellbeing through Music in Everyday Life*. Farnham, UK: Ashgate, 2013.

———. *Music in Everyday Life*. Cambridge: Cambridge University Press, 2000.

de Wit, Hans. "Globalization and Internationalization of Higher Education." *Revista de Universidad Sociedad del Conocimiento* 8, no. 2 (2011): 241–248.

Earley, P. Christopher, Charles Murnieks, and Elaine Mosakowski. "Cultural Intelligence and the Global Mindset." In *The Global Mindset*, edited by Mansour Javidan, Richard M. Steers, and Michael A. Hitt, 75–104. Oxford: JAI Elsevier, 2007.

Edwards, Richard, and Robin Usher. *Globalisation and Pedagogy: Space, Place and Identity*. London: Routledge, 2008.

Elliott, David J. *Music Matters: A New Philosophy of Music Education*. New York: Oxford University Press, 1995.

Elliott, David J., and Marissa Silverman. *Music Matters: A Philosophy of Music Education*. New York: Oxford University Press, 2014.

Elliott, David J., Marissa Silverman, and Wayne D. Bowman. *Artistic Citizenship: Artistry, Social Responsibility and Ethical Praxis*. New York: Oxford University Press, 2016.

El Sistema USA. "El Sistema in Venezuela." http://www.elsistemausa.org/el-sistema-in -venezuela.htm (accessed June 29, 2017).

Enslin, Penny, and Kai Horsthemke. "Can Ubuntu Provide a Model for Citizenship Education in African Democracies?" *Comparative Education* 40, no. 4 (2004): 545–558.

Epstein, Erwin H. "Comparative and International Education: Overview and Historical Development." In *The International Encyclopedia of Education*, vol. 2, 2nd ed., edited by Torsten Husen, 918–923. Oxford: Pergamon Press, 1994.

Eriksen, Thomas H. *Globalization*. London: Bloomsbury Academic, 2007.

Faure, Edgar, Filipe Herrera, Abdul-Razzak Kaddoura, Henri Lopes, Arthur V. Petrovsky, Majid Rahnema, and Frederick Champion Ward. *Learning to Be: The World of Education Today and Tomorrow*. Paris: UNESCO, 1972. http://unesdoc.unesco.org/images/0000/000018/001801e.pdf.

Feld, Steven. "My Life in the Bush of Ghosts: World Music and the Commodification of Religious Experience." In *Music and Globalization: Critical Encounters*, edited by Bob W. White, 40–51. Bloomington: Indiana University Press, 2012.

Finney, John, and Pamela Burnard. *Music Education with Digital Technology*. London: Continuum, 2007.

Firth, Alan. "The Discursive Accomplishment of Normality: On 'Lingua Franca' English and Conversation Analysis." *Journal of Pragmatics* 26 (1996): 237–259.

Fleer, Marilyn, Marianne Hedegaard, and Jonathan Tudge. *Childhood Studies and the Impact of Globalization: Policies and Practices at the Global and the Local Levels*. London: Routledge, 2009.

Fossum, Hanne, and Oivind Varkoy. "The Changing Concept of Aesthetic Experience in Music Education." *Nordic Research in Music Education Yearbook* 14 (2012): 9–25.

Foucault, Michel. *The Order of Things*. London: Tavistock, 1970.

Fowler, Sandra M., and Judith M. Blohm. "An Analysis for Methods of Intercultural Training." In *Handbook of Intercultural Training*, edited by Dan Landis, Janet M. Bennett, and Milton J. Bennett, 37–84. London: Sage, 2004.

Froehlich, Hildegard. "Music Education and Community: Reflections on 'Webs of Interaction' in School Music." *Action, Criticism and Theory for Music Education* 8, no. 1 (2009): 85–107. http://act.maydaygroup.org/articles/Froehlich8_1.pdf.

———. *A Social Theory for Music Education*. Lewiston, NY: Edwin Mellen, 2015.

Fullan, Michael, and Suzanne M. Stiegelbauer. *The New Meaning of Educational Change*. 2nd ed. London: Cassell, 1996.

Garnett, James. "Young People's Experiences of Learning Music in Other Countries." In *Listen Out: International Perspectives on Music Education*, edited by Chris Harrison and Sarah Hennessy, 74–77. Solihull, UK: National Association of Music Educators, 2012.

Glover, Jerry, and Harris L. Friedman. *Transcultural Competence: Navigating Cultural Differences in the Global Community*. Washington, DC: American Psychological Association, 2015.

Goehr, Lydia. *The Imaginary Museum of Musical Works: An Essay in the Philosophy of Music*. Oxford, UK: Clarendon Press, 1992.

Green, Lucy. *How Popular Musicians Learn: A Way Ahead for Music Education*. Aldershot, UK: Ashgate, 2001.

———. *Learning, Teaching, and Musical Identity*. Bloomington: Indiana University Press, 2011.

———. *Music, Informal Learning and the School: A New Classroom Pedagogy*. Farnham, UK: Ashgate, 2009.

Gruhn, Wilfried. "European 'Methods' for American Nineteenth-Century Singing Instruction: A Cross-Cultural Perspective on Historical Research." *Journal of Historical Research in Music Education* 23, no. 1 (2001): 3–18.

Hall, Edward T. *Beyond Culture*. Garden City, NY: Anchor, 1976.

Hall, Stuart. "The Local and the Global: Globalization and Ethnicity." In *Culture, Globalization and the World System*, edited by Anthony D. King, 19–40. Minneapolis: University of Minnesota Press, 1997.

Halls, Wilfried D. *Comparative Education: Contemporary Issues and Trends*. London: Jessica Kingsley, 1990.

Harrison, Chris, and Sarah Hennessy, eds. *Listen Out: International Perspectives on Music Education*. Solihull, UK: National Association of Music Educators, 2012.

Haywood, Terry. "A Simple Typology of International-Mindedness and Its Implications for Education." In *The Sage Handbook of Research in International Education*, edited by Mary Hayden, Jack Levy, and Jeff Thompson, 79–89. London: Sage, 2007.

Hebert, David G., and Alexandra Kertz-Welzel. *Patriotism and Nationalism in Music Education*. Farnham, UK: Ashgate, 2012.

Hébert, Yvonne, and Ali A. Abdi, eds. *Critical Perspectives on International Education*. Rotterdam, Netherlands: Sense, 2013.

Hentschke, Liane. "Global Policies and Local Needs in Music Education in Brazil." *Arts Education Policy Review* 114 (2013): 119–125.

Hess, Juliet. "Performing Tolerance and Curriculum: The Politics of Self-Congratulation, Identity Formation, and Pedagogy in World Music Education." *Philosophy of Music Education Review* 21, no. 1 (2013): 66–91.

Ho, Wai-chung. *Popular Music, Cultural Politics and Music Education in China*. London: Routledge, 2017.

———. *School Music Education and Social Change in Mainland China, Hong Kong and Taiwan*. Leiden, Netherlands: Brill, 2011.

Hofstede, Geert. *Culture's Consequences: Comparing Values, Behaviours, Institutions and Organizations across Nations*. London: Sage, 2003.

Hofstede, Geert, Gert Jan Hofstede, and Michael Minkov. *Cultures and Organizations: Software of the Mind*. New York: McGraw-Hill, 2004.

Holmes, Brian. "Comparative Education." In *The Encyclopedia of Education*, edited by Lee C. Deighton, 357–363. New York: Macmillan, 1971.

———. *Comparative Education: Some Considerations of Method*. London: George Allen and Unwin, 1981.

———. *Problems in Education*. London: Routledge, 1965.

Hopkins, Anthony G. *Globalization in World History*. New York: W. W. Norton, 2002.

Horckheimer, Max, and Theodor W. Adorno. *Dialectic of Enlightenment*, translated by Edmund Jephcott. Stanford, CA: Stanford University Press, 2002.

Horsley, Stephanie. "A Comparative Analysis of Neoliberal Education Reform and Music Education in England and Ontario, Canada." PhD diss., University of Western Ontario, 2014. http://ir.lib.uwo.ca/cgi/viewcontent.cgi?article=3204&context=etd.

Hughes, Robert Edward. *Schools at Home and Abroad*. London: Swan Sonnenschein, 1901.

Hyland, Ken. *Academic Publishing: Issues and Challenges in the Construction of Knowledge*. Oxford: Oxford University Press, 2015.

———. *Disciplinary Identities: Individuality and Community in Academic Discourse*. Cambridge: Cambridge University Press, 2012.

International Commission on Education for the Twenty-First Century. *Learning: The Treasure Within*. Paris: UNESCO, 1996. http://unesdoc.unesco.org/images/0010/001095/109590eo.pdf.

"Internationalization." *Business Dictionary.* http://www.businessdictionary.com/defini
tion/internationalization.html (accessed June 28, 2017).

James, Allison, and Adrian James. *Key Concepts in Childhood Studies.* London: Sage, 2012.

Javidan, Mansour, Richard M. Steers, and Michael A. Hitt. *The Global Mindset.* Oxford:
JAI Elsevier, 2007.

Jellison, Judith A. *Including Everyone: Creating Music Classrooms Where All Children
Learn.* New York: Oxford University Press, 2015.

Jenkins, Jennifer. *English as Lingua Franca in the International University: The Politics of
Academic English Language Policy.* New York: Routledge, 2014.

Jones, Patrick M. "Music Education for Society's Sake: Music Education in an Era of Global
Neo-imperial/Neo-medieval Market-Driven Paradigms and Structures." *Action,
Criticism and Theory for Music Education* 6, no. 1 (2007): 2–28. http://act.mayday
group.org/articles/Jones6_1.pdf.

———. "Returning Music Education to the Mainstream: Reconnecting with the Community." *Visions of Research in Music Education* 7 (January 2006). http://users.rider
.edu/~vrme/v7n1/visions/Jones%20Returning%20Music%20Education%20to%20
the%20Mainstream.pdf.

———. "Why We Need Policy Research in Music Education and What We Can Do to
Create an Impactful Policy Community in and for Music Education." In *Policy and
Media in and for a Diverse Global Community,* edited by Peter Gouzouasis, 85–92.
Vancouver: University of British Columbia, 2014. http://issuu.com/official_isme
/docs/2014_isme_policy_procedings/1?e=1871 006/8519907.

Jorgensen, Estelle R. *Pictures of Music Education.* Bloomington: Indiana University Press,
2011.

———. *Transforming Music Education.* Bloomington: Indiana University Press, 2003.

———. "Western Classical Music and General Education." *Philosophy of Music Education
Review* 11, no. 2 (2003): 130–140.

Kamens, David H. "Globalization and the Emergence of an Audit Culture: PISA and the
Search for 'Best Practices' and Magic Bullets." In *PISA, Power and Policy: The Emergence of Educational Governance,* edited by Heinz-Dieter Mayer and Aaron Benavot, 117–140. Oxford: Symposium Books, 2013.

Kaplan, Robert. "Cultural Thought Patterns in Intercultural Education." *Language Learning* 16, no. 1 (1966): 1–20.

Kefalas, Asterios G. "Think Globally, Act Locally." *Thunderbird International Business
Review* 40, no. 6 (1998): 547–562.

Kemp, Anthony E., and Laurence Lepherd. "Research Methods in International and
Comparative Music Education." In *Handbook of Research on Music Teaching and
Learning,* edited by Richard Colwell, 773–788. New York: Schirmer, 1992.

Kennedy, Michael D. *Globalizing Knowledge.* Stanford, CA: Stanford University Press,
2015.

Kerr, Clark. *The Uses of the University.* 5th ed. Cambridge, MA: Harvard University Press,
2001.

Kertz-Welzel, Alexandra. "Didaktik of Music: A German Concept and Its Comparison to
American Music Pedagogy." *International Journal of Music Education (Practice)* 22,
no. 3 (2004): 277–286.

———. *Every Child for Music: Musikunterricht und Musikpaedagogik in den USA* [Every
child for music: Music education in the United States]. Essen, Germany: Blaue Eule,
2006.

———. "Internationalisierung und musikpaedagogische Wissenschaftskulturen: Eine Annaeherung" [Internationalization and academic culture in music education: An approach]. *Zeitschrift fuer Kritische Musikpaedagogik* [Journal of critical music education] 3 (2015): 35–48. http://zfkm.org/sonder15-kertz-welzel.pdf.

———. "Lesson Learned? In Search of Patriotism and Nationalism in the German Music Education Curriculum." In *Patriotism and Nationalism in Music Education*, edited by David G. Hebert and Alexandra Kertz-Welzel, 23–42. Farnham, UK: Ashgate, 2012.

———. "Lessons from Elsewhere? Comparative Music Education in Times of Globalization." *Philosophy of Music Education Review* 23, no. 1 (2015): 48–66.

———. "Multicultural or Intercultural? The Impact of Political Conceptions on Music Education Approaches in Germany and the United States." Paper presented at the 8th International RIME (Research in Music Education) Conference, Exeter, UK, April 9–13, 2013.

———. "Music Education in the 21st Century: A Comparison of German and American Music Education Toward a New Concept of Global Exchange." *Music Education Research* 10, no. 4 (2008): 439–449.

———. "Musikpaedagogische Grundbegriffe und die Internationalisierung der Musikpaedagogik: Ein unloesbares Dilemma?" [Basic ideas in music education and internationalization: An insoluble dilemma?]. In *(Grund-)Begriffe musikpaedagogischen Nachdenkens: Entstehung, Bedeutung, Gebrauch* [Basic ideas in music education: Development, meaning, use], edited by Juergen Vogt, Frauke Hess, and Markus Brenk, 19–35. Müenster, Germany: LIT, 2014.

———. "The Pied Piper of Hamelin: Adorno on Music Education." *Research Studies in Music Education* 25, no. 1 (2005): 1–12.

———. "Revisiting Bildung and Its Meaning for International Music Education Policy." In *Policy and the Political Life of Music Education*, edited by Patrick Schmidt and Richard Colwell, 107–121. New York: Oxford University Press, 2017.

———. "The Singing Muse?" *Journal of Historical Research in Music Education* 26, no. 1 (2004): 8–27.

———. "Sociological Implications of English as an International Language in Music Education." *Action, Criticism and Theory for Music Education* 15, no. 3 (2016): 53–66. http://act.maydaygroup.org/articles/KertzWelzel15_3.pdf.

———. "Transcultural Childhoods." in *The Child as Musician*. 2nd ed., edited by Gary E. McPherson, 577–593. Oxford: Oxford University Press, 2016.

———. "'Two Souls, Alas, Reside within My Breast': Reflections on German and American Music Education Regarding the Internationalization of Music Education." *Philosophy of Music Education Review* 21, no. 1 (2013): 52–65.

Kiwan, Nadia, and Ulrike Hanna Meinhof. *Cultural Globalization and Music: African Artists in Transnational Networks*. New York: Palgrave Macmillan, 2011.

Knight, Jane. "Five Myths about Internationalization." *International Higher Education*, no. 62 (2011): 14–15. http://ecahe.eu/w/images/d/d5/Knight_-_Five_myths_about_Internationalization_-_IHE_no_62_Winter_2011.pdf.

———. "Five Truths about Internationalization." *International Higher Education*, no. 69 (2012). http://ejournals.bc.edu/ojs/index.php/ihe/article/view/8644/7776.

———. "Updating the Definition of Internationalization." *International Higher Education*, no. 33 (2003). https://www.bc.edu/content/dam/files/research_sites/cihe/pdf/IHEpdfs/ihe33.pdf.

Kok, Roe-Min. "Music for a Postcolonial Child: Theorizing Malaysian Memories." In *Learning, Teaching and Musical Identity*, edited by Lucy Green, 73–90. Bloomington: Indiana University Press, 2011.

Kroehl, Rixa Regina. *Change Management*. Konstanz, Germany: UVK, 2016.

Langer, Susanne K. *Philosophy in a New Key*. New York: New American Library, 1957.

Lathrop, Tad. *This Business of Global Music Marketing*. New York: Billboard Books, 2007.

Leung, Chi Cheung. "A Theoretical Framework on Effective Implementation of Music/Arts Education Policy in Schools." In *Music Education Policy and Implementation: International Perspectives*, edited by Chi Cheung Leung, Lai Chi Rita Yip, and Tadahiko Imada, 8–17. Hirosaki, Japan: Hirosaki University Press, 2008.

Levin, Benjamin. "An Epidemic of Education Policy: (What) Can We Learn from Each Other?" *Comparative Education* 34, no. 2 (1998): 131–141.

Lillis, Theresa, and Mary Jane Curry. *Academic Writing in a Global Context*. London: Routledge, 2010.

Mak, Peter. "Formal, Non-formal and Informal Learning in Music." In *Vom wilden Lernen* [About wild learning], edited by Peter Roebke and Natalie Ardilla-Mantilla, 31–44. Mainz, Germany: Schott, 2009.

Mark, Michael L., and Patrice Madura. *Contemporary Music Education*. London: Wadsworth, 2013.

Marsh, Kathryn. *The Musical Playground: Global Tradition and Changes in Children's Songs and Games*. New York: Oxford University Press, 2008.

———. "Music in the Lives of Refugee and Newly Arrived Immigrant Children in Sydney, Australia." In *The Oxford Handbook of Children's Musical Cultures*, edited by Patricia Shehan Campbell and Trevor Wiggins, 429–509. Oxford: Oxford University Press, 2013.

Martin, Denis-Constant. "The Musical Heritage of Slavery: From Creolization to World Music." In *Music and Globalization: Critical Encounters*, edited by Bob W. White, 17–39. Bloomington: Indiana University Press, 2012.

Mauranen, Anna. "Cultural Differences in Academic Discourse: Problems of a Linguistic and Cultural Minority." In *The Competent Intercultural Communicator*, edited by L. Löfman, L. Kurki-Suonio, S. Pellinen, and J. Lehtonen, 157–174. Jyväskylä: Finnish Association of Applied Linguistics, 1993. http://www.afinla.fi/sites/afinla.fi/files/1993Mauranen.pdf.

Mauranen, Anna, Carmen Perez-Llantada, and John M. Swales. "Academic Englishes: A Standardized Knowledge?" In *The Routledge Handbook of World Englishes*, edited by Andy Kirkpatrick, 634–652. New York: Routledge, 2010.

McCarthy, Marie. "International Perspectives." In *The Oxford Handbook of Music Education*, vol. 1, edited by Gary E. McPherson and Graham F. Welch, 40–62. New York: Oxford University Press, 2012.

———. *Toward a Global Community: The International Society for Music Education, 1953–2003*. Nedlands: Callaway International Resource Centre for Music Education, University of Western Australia, 2004.

McPherson, Gary E. *The Child as Musician: A Handbook of Musical Development*. 2nd ed. Oxford: Oxford University Press, 2016.

McPherson, Gary E., and Graham F. Welch. *Oxford Handbook of Music Education*. 2 vols. Oxford: Oxford University Press, 2012.

Merkt, Irmgard. *Deutsch-tuerkische Musikpaedagogik in der Bundesrepublik: ein Situationsbericht* [German-Turkish music education in Germany: A situation report]. Essen, Germany: Express Edition, 1983.

Meyer, Heinz-Dieter, and Aaron Benavot. "PISA and the Globalization of Educational Governance: Some Puzzles and Problems." In *PISA, Power and Policy: The Emergence of Educational Governance*, edited by Heinz-Dieter Mayer and Aaron Benavot, 7–26. Oxford: Symposium Books, 2013.

Myers, David E. "Freeing Music Education from Schooling: Toward a Lifespan Perspective on Music Learning and Teaching." *International Journal of Community Music* 1, no. 1 (2007): 49–61. http://www.intellectbooks.co.uk/MediaManager/Archive/IJCM/Volume%20D/03%20Myers.pdf.

Noah, Harold J. "Comparative Education: Methods." In *The Encyclopedia of Comparative Education and National Systems of Education*, edited by T. Neville Postlethwaite, 869–872. Oxford: Pergamon Press, 1988.

Noah, Harold J., and Max A. Eckstein. *Toward a Science of Comparative Education*. London: Macmillan, 1969.

Nsamenang, A. Bame. "Cultures in Early Childhood Care and Education." In *Childhood Studies and the Impact of Globalization: Policies and Practices at the Global and Local Levels*, edited by Marilyn Fleer, Marianne Hedegaard, and Jonathan Tudge, 23–45. London: Routledge, 2009.

Ochs, Kimberly, and David Phillips. "Processes of Educational Borrowing in Historical Context." In *Educational Policy Borrowing: Historical Perspectives*, edited by David Phillips and Kimberly Ochs, 7–24. Oxford: Symposium Books, 2004.

O'Flynn, John. "National Identity and Music in Transition: Issues of Authenticity in a Global Setting." In *Music, National Identity and the Politics of Location: Between the Global and the Local*, edited by Ian Biddle and Vanessa Knights, 19–38. Aldershot, UK: Ashgate, 2007.

Ogawa, Masafumi. "Japan: Music as a Tool for Moral Education?" In *The Origins and Foundations of Music Education*, edited by Gordon Cox and Robin Stevens, 205–220. London: Continuum, 2010.

Ogusu, Tomoko. "Teaching Music in Different Cultural Contexts." In *Listen Out: International Perspectives on Music Education*, edited by Chris Harrison and Sarah Hennessy, 47–55. Solihull, UK: National Association of Music Educators, 2012.

Osterhammel, Juergen. *Geschichte der Globalisierung* [History of globalization]. Munich: Beck, 2007.

———. "Globale Horizonte europaeischer Kunstmusik, 1869–1930" [Global perspectives of Western European art music, 1869–1930]. *Geschichte und Gesellschaft* [History and society] 38 (2012): 86–132.

Parquette, Jonathan. "Theories of Professional Identity: Bringing Cultural Policy in Perspective." In *Cultural Policy, Work and Identity: The Creation, Renewal and Negotiation of Professional Subjectivities*, edited by Jonathan Parquette, 1–24. Farnham, UK: Ashgate, 2012.

Phillips, David. "Aspects of Educational Transfer." In *International Handbook of Comparative Education*, edited by Robert Cowen and Andreas M. Kazamias, 1061–1077. Dordrecht, Netherlands: Springer, 2009.

———. "Policy Borrowing in Education: Frameworks for Analysis." In *International Handbook on Globalization, Education and Policy Research*, edited by Joseph Zajda, 23–34. Dordrecht, Netherlands: Springer, 2005.

———. "Towards a Theory of Policy Attraction in Education." In *The Global Politics of Borrowing and Lending*, edited by Gita Steiner-Khamsi, 54–68. New York: Teachers College Press, 2004.

Phillips, David, and Michele Schweisfurth. *Comparative and International Education: An Introduction to Theory, Methods, and Practice.* London: Continuum, 2007.

Phillipson, Robert. *English-Only Europe? Challenging Language Policy.* New York: Routledge, 2003.

Pitts, Stephanie E. *Chances and Choices: Exploring the Impact of Music Education.* New York: Oxford University Press, 2012.

———. "Fostering Lifelong Engagement in Music." In *The Child as Musician*, 2nd ed., edited by Gary E. McPherson, 639–654. Oxford: Oxford University Press 2016.

Pitzer, Robert. "Youth Music at the Yakama Tribal School." In *The Oxford Handbook of Children's Musical Cultures*, edited by Patricia Shehan Campbell and Trevor Wiggins, 46–60. Oxford: Oxford University Press, 2013.

Popkewitz, Thomas. "Foreword." In *The Global Politics of Educational Borrowing and Lending*, edited by Gita Steiner-Khamsi, vii–xii. New York: Teachers College Press, 2004.

Postlethwaite, T. Neville. "Preface." In *The Encyclopedia of Comparative Education and National Systems of Education*, edited by T. Neville Postlethwaite, xvii–xxvii. Oxford: Pergamon Press 1988.

Potts, Patricia. "The Place of Experience in Comparative Education Research." In *Comparative Education Research: Approaches and Methods*, edited by Mark Bray, Bob Adamson, and Mark Mason, 63–82. Hong Kong: Springer 2007.

Quadros, André de, ed. *Many Seeds, Different Flowers: The Music Education Legacy of Carl Orff.* Nedlands: Callaway International Resource Centre for Music Education, University of Western Australia, 2000.

Rainbow, Bernarr. "The Land with Music: Reality and Myth in Music Education." In *Bernarr Rainbow on Music*, edited by Peter Dickinson, 174–183. Suffolk, UK: Boydell Press, 2012.

Rappleye, Jeremy. *Educational Transfer in an Era of Globalization: Theory-History-Comparison.* New York: Peter Lang, 2012.

Roudometof, Victor. *Glocalization: A Critical Introduction.* London: Routledge, 2016.

Rust, Val D. "Foreign Influences in Educational Reform." In *Cross-National Attraction in Education: Accounts from England and Germany*, edited by Hubert Ertl, 23–34. Oxford: Symposium Books, 2006.

Saether, Eva, Alagi Mbye, and Reza Shayestehe. "Intercultural Tensions and Creativity in Music." In *The Oxford Handbook of Music Education*, vol. 2, edited by Gary E. McPherson and Graham F. Welsh, 354–370. New York: Oxford University Press, 2012.

Sarath, Edward, David Myers, Patricia Shehan Campbell. *Redefining Music Studies in an Age of Change: Creativity, Diversity, Integration.* New York: Routledge, 2017.

Sartori, Giovanni. "Compare Why and How: Comparing, Miscomparing and the Comparative Method." In *Comparing Nations: Concepts, Strategies, Substance*, edited by Mattei Dogan and Ali Kazancigil, 14–34. Oxford: Blackwell 1994.

Scheuermann, William. "Globalization." In *Stanford Encyclopedia of Philosophy*, Summer 2010 ed. http://plato.stanford.edu/archives/sum2010/entries/globalization.

Schippers, Huib. *Facing the Music: Shaping Music Education from a Global Perspective.* New York: Oxford University Press, 2010.

Schippers, Huib, and Catherine Grant. *Sustainable Futures for Music Cultures: An Ecological Perspective.* New York: Oxford University Press, 2016.

Schmidt, Patrick. "Cosmopolitanism and Policy: A Pedagogical Framework for Global Issues in Music Education." *Arts Education Policy Review* 114 (2013): 103–111.

———. "Why Policy Matters: Developing a Policy Vocabulary within Music Education." In *Policy and the Political Life of Music Education*, edited by Patrick Schmidt and Richard Colwell, 11–36. New York: Oxford University Press, 2017.

Schneider, Anne Larason, and Helen Ingram. *Policy Design for Democracy*. Lawrence: University Press of Kansas, 1997.

Schriewer, Juergen. "Globalization in Education: Process and Discourse." *Policy Futures in Education* 1, no. 2 (2003): 271–283.

Schroeder, Johanne. "Crossing Borders, Closing Gaps: In Favour of European Student Exchange in Music Education." In *Listen Out: International Perspectives on Music Education*, edited by Chris Harrison and Sarah Hennessy, 14–19. Solihull, UK: National Association of Music Educators, 2012.

Sellar, Sam, and Bob Lingard. "PISA and the Expanding Role of OECD in Global Educational Governance." In *PISA, Power and Policy: The Emergence of Educational Governance*, edited by Heinz-Dieter Mayer and Aaron Benavot, 185–206. Oxford: Symposium Books, 2013.

Siebert, Daniel. *Musik im Zeitalter der Globalisierung: Prozesse, Perspektiven, Stile* [Music in the age of globalization: Processes, perspectives, styles]. Bielefeld, Germany: Transcript, 2015.

Srinivas, Kalburgi M. "Globalization of Business and the Third World." *Journal of Management Development* 14, no. 3 (1995): 26–49.

Steiner-Khamsi, Gita. "Transferring Education, Displacing Reform." In *Discourse Formation in Comparative Education*, edited by Juergen Schriewer, 110–132. Frankfurt, Germany: Peter Lang, 2000.

———. "Understanding Policy Borrowing and Lending: Building Comparative Policy Studies." In *World Yearbook of Education 2012: Policy Borrowing and Lending in Education*, edited by Gita Steiner-Khamsi and Florian Waldow, 3–17. New York: Routledge, 2012.

Stromquist, Nelly P. "Comparative and International Education: A Journey towards Equality and Equity." *Harvard Educational Review* 75, no. 1 (2005): 89–11.

Tan, Charlene, and Leonard Tan. "A Shared Vision of Human Excellence: Confucian Spirituality and Arts Education." *Pastoral Care in Education* 34, no. 3 (2016): 156–166.

Taylor, Timothy D. "World Music Today." In *Music and Globalization: Critical Encounters*, edited by Bob W. White, 172–188. Bloomington: Indiana University Press, 2012.

Thielmann, Winfried. *Deutsche und englische Wissenschaftssprache im Vergleich: Hinfuehren, Verknuepfen, Benennen* [A comparison of German and English academic language: Introducing, relating, designating]. Heidelberg, Germany: Synchron, 2009.

Thompson, Jeff. "International Education: Towards a Shared Understanding." *Journal of Research in International Education* 1, no. 1 (2002): 5–8.

Torres-Santos, Raymond. *Music Education in the Caribbean and Latin America: A Comprehensive Guide*. Lanham, MD: Rowman and Littlefield, 2017.

Trompenaars, Fons. "Foreword." In Jerry Glover and Harris L. Friedman, *Transcultural Competence: Navigating Cultural Differences in the Global Community*. Washington, DC: American Psychological Association, 2015.

Trompenaars, Fons, and Charles Hampden-Turner. *Riding the Waves of Culture: Understanding Cultural Diversity in Business*. New York: McGraw-Hill, 1998.

Tunstall, Tricia. *Changing Lives: Gustavo Dudamel, El Sistema, and the Transformative Power of Music.* New York: W. W. Norton, 2012.

United Nations. "Convention on the Rights of the Child." November 20, 1989. http://www.ohchr.org/EN/ProfessionalInterest/Pages/CRC.aspx.

———. "Official Languages." http://www.un.org/en/sections/about-un/official-languages/index.html (accessed June 29, 2017).

———. "UN Secretary-General Launches Major New Education Initiative." September 26, 2012. http://iif.un.org/content/un-secretary-general-launches-major-new-education-initiative.

United Nations Educational, Scientific, and Cultural Organization. *Rethinking Education: Towards a Global Common Good?* Paris: UNESCO, 2015. http://unesdoc.unesco.org/images/0023/002325/232555e.pdf.

———. "Road Map for Arts Education." 2006. http://www.unesco.org/new/fileadmin/MULTIMEDIA/HQ/CLT/CLT/pdf/Arts_Edu_RoadMap_en.pdf.

Väkevä, Lauri, Cathy Benedict, Patrick Schmidt, Geir Johansen, and Alexandra Kertz-Welzel. "Four Pieces on Comparative Philosophy of Music Education." *Philosophy of Music Education Review* 21, no. 1 (2013): 5–7. http://muse.jhu.edu/journals/philosophy_of_music_education_review/toc/pme.21.1.html.

Wallis, Roger, and Krister Malm. *Big Sounds from Small People: The Music Industry in Small Countries.* London: Constable, 1984.

Wells, Karen. *Childhood in a Global Perspective.* Cambridge, UK: Polity, 1999.

Welsch, Wolfgang. "Transculturality—the Puzzling Form of Cultures Today." In *Spaces of Culture: City, Nation, World*, edited by Mike Featherstone and Scott Lash, 194–213. London: Sage, 1999. http://www2.uni-jena.de/welsch/papers/W_Wlelsch_Transculturality.html.

White, Bob W. "Introduction: Rethinking Globalization through Music." In *Music and Globalization: Critical Encounters*, edited by Bob W. White, 1–16. Bloomington: Indiana University Press, 2012.

———. *Music and Globalization: Critical Encounters.* Bloomington: Indiana University Press, 2012.

———. "The Promise of World Music: Strategies for Non-essentialist Listening." In *Music and Globalization: Critical Encounters*, edited by Bob W. White, 189–218. Bloomington: Indiana University Press, 2012.

Wilson, David N. "Comparative and International Education: Fraternal or Siamese Twins? A Preliminary Genealogy of Our Twin Fields." *Comparative Education Review* 4 (November 1994): 449–486.

Wilton, Antje. "The Monster and the Zombie: English as a Lingua Franca and the Latin Analogy." *Journal of English as Lingua Franca* 1, no. 2 (2012): 337–364.

Wiseman, Alexander W., and David P. Baker. "The Worldwide Explosion of Internationalized Education Policy." In *Global Trends in Educational Policy*, edited by David P. Baker and Alexander W. Wiseman, 1–21. Amsterdam: Elsevier, 2005.

Woodford, Paul G. *Democracy and Music Education.* Bloomington: Indiana University Press, 2005.

———. *Re-thinking Standards for the Twenty-First Century: New Realities, New Challenges, New Propositions.* London: University of Western Ontario, 2011.

Zhou, Yuefang, Divya Jindal-Snape, Keith Topping, and John Todman. "Theoretical Models of Culture Shock and Adaptation in International Students in Higher Education." *Studies in Higher Education* 33, no. 1 (2008): 63–75.

Index

Abdi, Ali, 20
Abreu, José Antonio, 44
academia, 28
academic discourses, 11
academic field, comparative education as, 50
academic folklore, 53
academic goals, 38
academic language/writing, 30, 66–68, 70
academic rationales for internationalization, 21
academic text production, 7
Adams, John, 28
Adamson, Bob, 50
Adick, Christel, 23
administration, 37, 52, 80, 87
adults, 44, 89–90, 93–94
aesthetic experience, 27, 66
Afro-American music, 25
agency, 44, 85
amateurs, 57, 59
ambiguity, 89, 99
Anderson, Benedict, 62
Anglo-American model, 99; aesthetic education in, 67; of music education, 6, 9, 58, 61–62, 65, 67, 68, 70, 111; of research, 6, 70, 72; standards of, 11, 70; terminology of, 67; writing in, 70–72
Argentina, 43
arts, 8, 18, 81–83, 85, 87–88, 104
Asia, 65
assessment, 5, 19, 36–38, 48, 51–52, 74n21
Australia, 43, 86, 89
authenticity, 26, 92

Baker, David, 43
Bamford, Anne, 8, 88
Becher, Tony, 63
Bereday, George, 49–50, 51–52, 54
Bildung, 37–38, 42, 56, 66–67, 110n83
Bologna, 38–39
borrowing, 35–48, 50, 74n17, 74n21
Bowman, Wayne, 59–61
Brandenburg, Uwe, 10, 13, 21–22
Bray, Mark, 50–51, 53
Brazil, 8, 52, 87
British education model, 18, 32n22, 37–38, 43, 68
Burnard, Pamela, 93

Campbell, Patricia Shehan, 63, 90, 91–92
Canada, 8, 44
Canagarajah, Athelstan, 65, 114
Carney, Stephen, 48
characteristics: of childhood, 89; of disciplinary communities, 63; of language, 31; of music education, 7, 50, 59, 62–63; of a profession, 59
Cheng, Kai-Ming, 20
China, 7
citizens, 18, 22, 38, 57, 66, 105
citizenship, 17, 22–23, 112
Clark, Burton, 63
classical music, 27, 40–41, 43–44, 58, 60, 92
classroom: activities in, 27, 94; diversity in, 105; global music classroom, 11–12, 89, 93, 96; and internationalization, 21, 67; in multilevel analysis, 51; music education classroom, 6, 68, 86; and music education policy, 81; pedagogy in, 95; transformation in, 101; world music classroom, 92
colonialism, 28, 104
community music, 57, 94, 106
competencies, 26, 45, 56, 59, 80, 92, 94, 99; cross-cultural, 99; intercultural, 21, 98, 111; language, 72; scholarly, 71
competition, 36, 84
concert, 60
Coupland, Nikolas, 2, 3
Cowen, Robert, 48
Cox, Gordon, 7
creativity: in educational models, 68; and globalization, 20; linguistic, 31; musical, 89, 92, 93; music education and, 6, 58, 84, 95, 101, 105
cross-national attraction, 36–37, 40, 42, 44
curriculum: British piano, 43; development of, 57, 81–82; of El Sistema, 44; and informal learning, 95, 105; in multilevel analysis, 51; school, 57, 60, 87; transformation of, 20
Curry, Mary Jane, 70, 71–72
Curwen, John Spencer, 40, 74n17

Dalcroze method, 42–43, 58
Daly, Herman, 4

ALEXANDRA KERTZ-WELZEL is Professor and Department Chair of Music Education at Ludwig-Maximilians-Universität in Munich, Germany. She is the author or editor of several books, has published in leading journals, and has regularly presented at national and international conferences. She is currently chair of the International Society for the Philosophy of Music Education and cochair of the International Society for Music Education Commission on Policy.